TIERS OF SORROW

A true story of
Homicide,
Betrayal,
Courage,
and Hope

SANDRA TOSCANO

Published by Sandra Toscano
Pagination: Elevita Media
Photography: ShantayInk.com
Illustration: Austin Huerta

CONTENTS

DEDICATION

I want to dedicate this book to my son Andy and his wife Rosemary, my daughter Jennie and her husband Noah, and to my youngest son Austin; because together, we grieved through the depths of despair, suffering through months and years of agony trying to accept the death of our beloved Sergio Jr. United in a journey of survival and strengthening our bond along the way; while recognizing that we were not alone. May my love and eternal gratitude give you wings to fly further and reach higher; may you learn along the way that you can fulfill your dreams and that you have the potential to accomplish great things. Remember that giving up is not an option and that I will always be there for you.

May you find another layer of healing in the passages written in this book and may the Tiers of Sorrow that you have each suffered be mended by the healing hand of our most loving God.

—With all my love

FOREWORD

Victims and ex-offenders working together as a necessary component towards change in the world of violence

My daughter Samaya turned four years old on this particular day in Wisconsin. I was excited to get back to my room to talk with her over Skype. I was wrapping up a presentation at a statewide gang conference in August 2012. Lately my work has taken me around the globe trying to combat violent extremism. I have met victims from all over the world including victims of the London Tube Bombing, victims of the 9/11 attacks, victims of terror cell kidnappings, as well as the men and women who once participated in such hateful groups and acts.

Walking out of the conference room and into the main hall, I met Sandra Toscano. She was sitting at the table where I had been selling books about my life and the process of forgiveness. Now, on that same table were books about the life and death of her son Sergio. In the face of this tragic event I could not help but notice that Sandra looked stoic, and yet I knew that her pain ran deep. She explained that it takes intense prayer and focus to do these presentations because it is heartbreaking and emotionally draining to relive her son's death each time she presents on this topic. If you have ever been to any conference, you know that as you walk by all the tables you only half listen until you find a table that captures your interest. As I listened to Sandra, the gravity and seriousness of her situation, only outdone by the bizarre nature of events, was evident within just a few words. I started to feel weak in the knees. I asked if I could sit next to her and listen to her describe her experience.

The incredible nature of events that led to her son's homicide was by itself enough to cause a dense darkness to linger in the air. With each word that Sandra spoke, the uncanny parallels between me and the man who killed her son were screaming inside of my head. When she was done I asked if I could share something with her. She granted me her permission.

"I am sorry for what I have done. I used to be like the man who killed your son. I am ashamed. I want to help restore your faith in humanity by showing you that people like that can change," I said with tears rolling down my face.

"Thank you for saying that Sammy," she gently replied. "It is good to know that people like that can find their way out." Every word of kindness and understanding that she spoke cut deeper than the one before. Sandra had to get ready to present in just a few minutes. She was going into the same room that I had just exited to share her experience, strength, and her message with others.

An alleged member of a notorious gang killed this mom's son. I wanted to kneel before her and beg her forgiveness as if she could wipe away my sins. I wanted to run from her in my shame. I wanted her to slap me in my face and tell me how evil I am. I wanted to start punishing myself all over again. The hardest thing that any of us will ever do is to face ourselves in the mirrors that other spirits hold in front of us.

Leaving the conference feeling raw with guilt, remorse, shame, and empathy, I wrote the following thoughts as the plane was taking me back home to my family.

> Who am I in the face of what I have done in
> this world and the people in it? You should
> know I am stuck with that darkness as it is

written in my very DNA and beyond. I used to
be all-powerful and all-knowing. The only perfect people in this world are addicts and criminals; at least in our own addicted and criminal
minds. Who am I in the face of what I have
become as a result of living as a violent, cold,
hateful, murderous man? I don't deserve the
forgiveness that has been shown to me, but
that's what makes it so precious to give and to
receive.

Sandra had said to me, just before going on to share her life,
"Sammy, if I am to love my children the way they deserve, or do any
good in this world, or honor my son's life... I have to lay it all at the
feet of Jesus, I have to bring it to the Cross." she said holding back
the tears. "Forgiveness can be a long and painful process, and the
Lord is working in me on that as well," she said as she walked away,
trying to hide the tears that were now streaming down her face.

Who am I to be walking around free and at
peace while my victims live with the legacy of
my actions? I am not important. The people I
serve are important. The people I have hurt
are important. The work I do is important. But
me, I deserve to be living with my guilt and
shame.

But, something or someone has other plans for me. I have been
freed from the chains of hell, to walk freely in hell in order to free
others who would be like me. I am focused on the writ bestowed
upon me to confront my demons; so that I may help others do the

same. Rarely is it what I do that is difficult, but more so the belief that somehow the world would be better served if I remained chained and useless.

A man asked me one day if I had accepted Jesus Christ as my personal savior. Once I answered he told me I would burn in hell. Little did he know that from birth that's where I had been—in hell. I wish he knew I would gladly go back if it were what I owe. And beyond that, little did he know that hell is where I work every day and every night. My spirit has been tempered with flames and suffering. Who else could go to the depths of Hades with others to light the way out?

Who am I? I am the person I was created to be.

Victims and ex-offenders known as Formers working together; it is an unlikely, but ever so necessary duo and component towards effecting change in the world. I am always struck by the compassion emanating from victims of violence when they hear my story and about my own violent past. They choose to see the best in me and others like me, they give us their blessing and forgiveness even though they know, as well as I do, that we do not deserve it. It is a pure act of love and kindness, born from spirituality and compassion, stemming from their suffering by way of genuineness and incredible strength.

Sandra's book is the light that has escaped the black hole of violent extremism. This is a must read for anyone in the grief support field, those seeking healing and recovery from great loss and trauma, and for restorative justice groups, prisons, schools, and colleges, but also the person who thinks it can never happen to them. Just brushing against Sandra's life has sparked a never-ending desire to get involved and to do more. It will do even more for you.

In Loving Memory of all those lost to violence and hate.

—Sammy Rangel MSW, CSAC
Founder of Formers Anonymous
Author of *FourBears: Myths of Forgiveness*

PREFACE

While there have been many books written about grief and the death of a child, the truth is you will never be able to grasp that intense level of pain unless you have lost one of your own. If you have never experienced the loss of a child, my story will help you support others who are overcome by grief due to such a catastrophe. If, however, you have been stricken by this tragedy, I offer you my sincere condolences. The death of a child is the most devastating loss you will ever face. This book will provide the hope and the help that you are seeking.

Many books are available to make the grieving journey more bearable. Each author has a unique perspective. You may find that your method of grieving and your family's method are different and that's okay. We share common ways of coping with severe pain and tragedy. But we all have different levels of pain tolerance, and each of us will also have different ways of coping with grief. Each person should adopt coping mechanisms that work best for him/her. We may experience some similar stages during the grieving process; however we may experience them in a different order. Our personal life experiences and external influencing factors will make each grieving journey unique.

Why did I write this book? More than to bring another perspective to the grieving process, I endeavor to add an essential element, one that made the biggest impact in my life during the crucial months and years that followed the death of my son. My life changed suddenly when faced with a decision—in the midst of ongoing, unbearable grief—a decision that defined a new course of action that eventually redefined me as a person.

I know the painful difference of surviving the death of a loved one with God by my side and the devastation and hopelessness of trying to handle it on my own, without God's peace and strength. I have walked both paths. It takes courage and God's power to survive in either one but there is a stark difference between the two. With God, there is peace and hope.

I would like to share that at one point, I pondered how people far from God could ever survive such a loss and endure such crippling pain. God allowed me the opportunity to find out for myself, and it definitely brought me to a more severe level of pain; another tier in the dark and overwhelming tragedy that seemed insurmountable by all the contributing factors in our case and the destructive pain behind our story. I have personally experienced such devastating grief and sorrow. I draw the connection from a sermon that I heard a pastor give a long time ago on the topic of suffering, which gives validity to this message. The pastor had said that he believes those who are called to minister to hurting people have first been equipped by God, allowing them to experience pain for themselves in order to know the tragedy that we will speak of firsthand and develop an in-depth understanding of the fundamental aspect of grief captured in the essence of body, mind, and spirit. How else could someone understand wholeheartedly the raw pain that a person must go through unless they experienced it themselves? I believe it would be difficult for someone to speak of restoration unless that person knows intimately what each of the grieving stages is all about.

There is an undeniable connection that bereaved people have with each other. The impact and raw experience binds them in an amazing and unexplainable way. There are many experienced professionals available to provide counseling and I offer my gratitude to them for working in the area of grief support. I encourage every person grieving the loss of a loved one to find ways that will help them best, particularly during the initial stages when we are most vulnerable to the pain and shock, plus numerous other emotions that can throw us off our normal state of mind. Only the person who is grieving can know the extent of the help they need in order to survive. There is a whole host of helpful resources available that are geared specifically to the type of loss a person is experiencing. Contact any of the many agencies, professionals, and online resources that have been established for this specific purpose. There is no shame in reaching out for help. In fact, isn't that the advice we would give our loved ones who have passed if the circumstances were reversed?

I trust that there is a purpose for everything that happens in our lives—and that God is ultimately in control. No matter what happens in our lives, God can turn an act that was meant for evil into a purposeful and meaningful event that can help others and bring glory to His name. I also believe that God gives us the free will to decide what we will do with each trial and circumstance that we encounter.

What are you prepared to do with your tragedy? What kind of meaning will you give the cross you carry and how will this help you remember your loved one? How can you best represent to others the character of your loved one? And, most importantly, what representation of God are you prepared to render?

As I contemplated whether or not to write this book, compelling as it may be, I considered the best and worst possible outcomes; outcomes that could potentially bring adverse effects on my family's safety. I weighed the probable scenarios that could unfold if I used our real names. I prayed for God's guidance and wisdom that the words written in these pages would never be used against us or bring our family any more harm.

On the other hand, I want to help others grieving the loss of a child or loved one. I believe these efforts can bring hope and inspiration to help others make it through such a painful journey. I consulted with others who graciously gave me advice and valuable counsel. Ultimately, it was my daughter Jennie who was instrumental in helping me make the difficult decision to write this book. Her counsel to me was to follow my heart and to not let fear stop me from writing this book the way I need to and the way I feel God wants me to. I have come to the conclusion that if I feel in my heart the true calling from God and I do not surrender my will to fulfill His purpose, that I might someday regret not following through on that calling. It would be much easier to ignore the calling and play it safe, pretend like this was all a silly notion and go on with my life—or I could take another giant leap of faith and trust in the Lord to give me the wisdom and courage I would need to carry out this project and follow through to the end.

I am fully aware that some may dispute my story. It is my intention to be as transparent as possible and to state the truth to the best of my knowledge. This is my story shared from my perspective with my account of the facts. It is not intended to serve as a tool to expose anyone or to bring shame to any individual. In my heart, I wish to render my interpretation in efforts to shed light into the bigger problem of gang and domestic violence.

After many months of prayer, my conscience would not let me go through life knowing that fear could deter me from doing what I feel is important work. I will not let my son's killer or those that helped him, rob me of the opportunity to turn my misery into a ministry that could help others in their struggle. And, so, I have put into writing the passages that are carved in my heart, the sketches of what my soul feels and longs to reveal, knowing that only a parent that has gone through a similar loss can possibly understand. Only a grief so dark and deep can touch another's hurt and bring light and hope in the midst of their sorrow.

Chapter One

THE CHILD

He pulled the knife out of his heart. He shouldn't have, he should have left it there, someone should have stopped him from doing it but it was a reaction to having something foreign inside his chest—and he couldn't breath. He walked into the kitchen from outside under his own power and needed help. "I've been stabbed," he said. Outside people were screaming, some were fighting, and others were trying to escape the area before the police arrived. But that didn't matter now. When he pulled the knife out, his heart poured blood into his chest cavity. He collapsed to the floor and went into shock immediately. His organs began to fail—he began to fail. He laid there clutching and gasping for air. He whispered in between gasps, "I can't breath." He whispered again, "It hurts, it really hurts." Someone called 911, twice, but there would be no one coming to save him. Betrayed by a family member whose parting words to him were, "That's what you get," he whispered no more and died on the floor.

This is a story of loss, of deep dark grief. It's a story of violence and betrayal. However, it's also a story of courage, faith, family, and eternal love.

The child...Sergio, Jr. was just as any normal, healthy child should be; energetic, happy, and full of life. As a young man, he was strong, caring, brave, and certainly tenacious. We as parents, sometimes think back to all the love, care, and sleepless nights we endure when our child was ill and the relief we felt when they began to feel better. I recall some of the conversations I had with Sergio, Jr. that added to

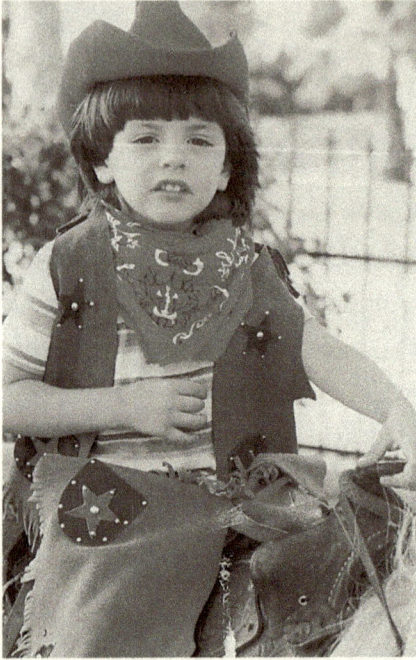

Sergio was our second born, and he grew up surrounded by a large family of six.

the strong bond we had, the special moments we shared that gave me insight into his being, and all the precious memories we made; some of which were captured in photos while others are stored in my heart...they are all real nonetheless, and so was he.

Many believe that when you are faced with death, your entire life flashes before your eyes. When I was told by the doctor that my son had died, his life flashed before me and I was struck with an immeasurable amount of pain.

Sergio was our second born; he grew up surrounded by a large family of six and an extended family that far exceeds one hundred. From the beginning, my husband and I have worked hard to raise our children with a good work ethic, with decency and integrity. I learned this work ethic from my mother, who worked endlessly to provide for us.

My father was unreliable at best—so my mother was basically a single mom who sacrificed everything to raise eleven children.

I witnessed her struggles and did not want to add to her load by asking for things. Instead, I felt the need to get a job and earn my own money. By the age of twelve I worked two jobs, delivering newspapers and working in my grandfather's restaurant. My mother allowed me to take on a paper route in our neighborhood. Although I hated getting up at five in the morning every Sunday, it was worth it. As the tallest girl in the family, all my hand-me-down jeans were much too short. I would never dream of asking my mother to buy longer pants that would only fit me, however, I was willing to earn the money to buy them myself.

After a few weeks of doing my route and learning my new business, my entrepreneurial spirit grew. I figured that if one person could get the route done in a given number of hours, then two could do it much faster. So I hired my younger brother Art. He was energetic and a quick study; but more importantly, he owned a bike! Once I got him trained, I shared the route with him and I took on an additional role, totally unrelated to the paper route. I began to work at my grandfather's restaurant on the weekends. It was a win-win for both me and my brother. Yes, I would have rather stayed home, watched cartoons, and just been a kid, but I enjoyed learning to be self-sufficient.

I learned other valuable lessons at that young age as well. At times, my mother would send two of us to our grandfather's restaurant to help him. While I loved helping Grandpa, it was strenuous work and not all of us carried the same work ethic. This became insufferable when I discovered the difference in pay that older siblings and I were receiving. In our culture it was typical to pay the older children more than the younger ones, regardless of the work load. Five years older, she was being paid twenty dollars per day while I was earning a mere ten. I, the ambitious worker, decided to do something about it.

I scouted the surrounding businesses for potential employment. I had made several contacts at the market next door while shopping for my grandpa, Papa Manuel. I felt I could start there. Now, I can't be sure, but I suspect Grandpa knew what I was up to and conspired with the store owner to teach me a lesson. I convinced the store

owner that I was a hard worker and a fast learner and could help at his store. He agreed to let me start the next day. When I told Mom about my new job, she was not happy. As I explained my reasons, she, for some odd reason, agreed to let me try.

When I arrived at the store, I was handed an apron, a price gun, and I was directed into the storage room where hundreds of boxes of merchandise waited to be priced. I worked endlessly. The store owner checked in on me from time to time and sometimes told me that I was doing a good job. I felt a great sense of accomplishment and at times thought to myself, "Maybe now, Grandpa will appreciate my hard work." The end of my shift at the store was drawing near and I was exhausted, but I was also looking forward to collecting my wages. I felt I had earned what I hoped would be a larger salary than what I received from my grandfather. Silly of me though, the store owner and I never discussed how much he would pay me. For some reason, I just figured it would be "fair." The store owner came in and told me that he was really happy with my work. He said that he realized that he dumped a lot on me on the first day but that I proved to be a good worker. He reached into his pocket, brought out a five dollar bill, and handed it to me. Then he asked if I would be back the next day. I was shocked. I wish I had video of that epic moment; I'm sure I would have won in a funniest video contest or a "sucker" competition. I was insulted and knew that I'd been taken. I learned to appreciate Grandpa and realized that I was not going to change my situation. I loved Grandpa and honestly enjoyed working with him. He was a man of few words, but he was a great man and everyone respected him. Needless to say, I was back at his establishment with a humble spirit and a greater appreciation for what I did earn. I loved knowing that my contribution lightened his burden, even if it was just on the weekends. My mom has told me that on several occasions Grandpa told her how much he appreciated the quality of my work. Those hard-earned compliments still warm my heart.

My husband and I have tried to teach our children the value of earning their own way and working hard. We have taught them the value of sacrifice and honesty, the value of an honorable reputation and that respect is earned. As any parent would, we helped pave the way for our children and worked hard to provide opportunities to shape their future, just as my mother did for my siblings and me. I am still amazed by my mother's resourcefulness and determination to raise her children well, despite the dire circumstances she endured over the years.

"Shh, shh, shh; hush little baby, don't say a word ..." I loved rock-ing my newborn baby to sleep while I whispered a lullaby, caressing his soft silky skin and watching him drift to sleep as I whispered "I love you." I named him Sergio, after his father. He grew up to become a strong-willed and confident boy with a great love for life. He was a strong and handsome young man who has now entered into a new realm, that of a blissful spiritual being; a new creation in Christ.

Sergio and his siblings were very close, and each of them went to great lengths to be there for one other. Andy, the firstborn, enjoyed being the sole recipient of my affections; however, his reign as an only child was short-lived. Sergio was born just a year later. Andy was a great big brother right from the beginning. He loved Sergio, but I can also think of countless times when Andy played pranks on his younger brother. As charming and witty as Andy was—and continues to be— teaching Sergio who was boss in their relationship was Andy's mission for the first few years. Though I must admit that not all the pranks deserved chastising, there were times when I was amazed at

Andy's capability to think outside the box.

I fondly remember an incident that happened when Andy was only eighteen months old and Sergio was six months old. I had stepped out of the kitchen for a few minutes to get the laundry from the next room and when I came back, I found Sergio covered in sugar. Andy was standing next to him—empty bag in hand—giggling as he celebrated his clever stunt. Sergio quickly caught on; he became very astute at self-defense and carried this characteristic well for the rest of his life.

Sergio's teenage years were those of a young man trying to make his mark in this world; he would often say to me, "Life is short; you have to live it fully." And that he did; he didn't take anything for granted. Sergio made me proud in many ways; he loved his family and would stand up to protect us. Ironically, this admirable trait led to his

Sergio bending down to talk to a little boy during a mission trip to the poor in Mexico.

death at the young age of twenty-one. Sergio was courageous and had a magnetic personality. Our family describes him as having the courage of a lion, the spirit of a warrior, and a heart of gold.

My husband and I provided for our children as best we could and even found ways to take them on mini vacations. Always on a very tight budget but we wanted them to experience new things, to see new places, and marvel at God's creation even if we had to pack a lunch and camp out. The pictures of those trips are now such treasured memories because we did them together; and there are some fabulous stories behind them all.

Sergio liked children and enjoyed being around them. When he got older, he volunteered to go on a mission trip with us to Mexico where we gave food and clothing to families in one of the worst poverty-stricken neighborhoods. I remember the distressed look on Sergio's face when he saw the living conditions that those poor peopled lived in. With tears in his eyes, he turned to me and hugged me; and then he whispered, "We are so blessed, Mom." I still keep the pictures of him and his sister Jennie from that trip. In one of these pictures, he is bending down talking to a little boy that caught his attention. He asked me to take a picture because he wanted to keep the photo of that little boy and capture the memory of that experience. It warmed my heart to see how much love he gave those children and it blessed me to see his humbleness; he said he considered himself no more than they.

I would, of course, be remiss if I didn't also tell you that Sergio could charm the ladies. He didn't date any particular girl for a prolonged period of time, but he was good to them and they seemed to enjoy his company. I could think of only a couple of girls that I believe he may have had deep feelings for. I remember a time when

he asked if he could take his younger brother Austin to the beach. Sergio explained that his girlfriend would accompany them and that he would have his brother back before nightfall. Austin excitedly jumped into the back seat and strapped on his seat belt; he loved spending time with his siblings and this was one of those special occasions where he could spend time with his older brother Sergio.

When they returned, I was surprised to see that Austin was now in the front seat of the car and Sergio's girlfriend was in the back. I asked Austin if they enjoyed their time at the beach and he replied that Sergio and his girlfriend had gotten into an argument on the way home. I glanced over to Sergio; he didn't say anything at first, but then reluctantly shared why Austin and his girlfriend had played musical chairs on the way home. In a low tone, he said to me that his girlfriend had not been happy that Austin had come along, but she had not said anything until they arrived at the beach. It appeared that things just

Sergio had a great sense of humor. During a trip to San Francisco he wanted his picture taken with these transients.

went south from there, to the point that, according to Sergio, she had been very rude to Austin. Sergio explained that after several attempts to get her to be civil during the ride home, he finally felt the need to pull over and have her switch seats with Austin, which of course, marked the end of that relationship. He very firmly told me that he would not allow anyone to be rude and mean to a little kid, and especially not to his little brother.

In 2003, during the last family vacation we took together, we toured San Francisco. By this time, Sergio was already twenty years old. Aside from his kind heart, Sergio also had a great sense of humor. As we walked along the sidewalks, we noticed a couple of transients holding up a sign that read, "Why lie? It's for beer." Sergio thought this was the funniest thing. He gave them credit for their creativity and honesty and he chuckled as he said, "This is awesome, I have to help them out." After donating to their beer fund, with the men's permission, Sergio posed with them for a photo. That picture is a testimony of our last vacation together and a witness to his kind heart and happy spirit.

On that same vacation we also toured Alcatraz. We enjoyed each other's company on the boat ride to the prison. Once inside, we found the living conditions in that prison quite deplorable; it gave us a glimpse as to the types of individuals that once occupied those jail cells. We gained insight into what the prisoners' lives must have been like and the horrible crimes they must have committed to warrant their imprisonment. As we toured the prison, the musty smell was undeniable and the cold clammy feel made me shiver. At the end of the tour, we saw a former Alcatraz inmate and author, selling his books. He agreed to take a picture with Sergio, and that too has become part of the collection of memories of that very special trip.

Sergio was definitely a straight shooter; he was blunt and honest about his perspectives. He didn't pretend to be something he wasn't, or pretend to like something when he didn't. He was a man of few words, but when asked, he would give you an honest answer— whether you liked it or not. He didn't sugarcoat his responses but was tactful in his choice of words because he didn't like to hurt anyone's feelings.

Because Sergio had been in high school just a few years before his sister Jennie, he became quite familiar with the lay of the land by the time she came to enter what he called, "the wolves den." Sergio had endured several bad experiences while in high school—being jumped by gang members on the first day for example, that he felt the need to be vigilant for his sister's safety. This cramped her style as it often interfered with her social life. Later that year, Sergio exposed a situation that Jennie had tried to keep secret.

My reading was interrupted by the sound of loud voices coming from the living room. Jennie complained that Sergio was crossing the line by interfering with her choice of friends. Sergio explained that this particular group of friends was not a good influence, and more specifically, a certain guy that she had been hanging out with was bad news. Jennie couldn't believe that Sergio was even aware of these things. She asked him point blank, "How do you know about all this?" To which Sergio replied, "I know what I know, because I make it my business to be informed of anything that would affect my family." Once Jennie understood that Sergio only had her best interests at heart, they were able to resolve the situation. She never again doubted his love for her. They were close despite their six-year age gap.

I grew up in a home with an alcoholic father and a mother that worked endlessly to provide for us. She endured physical, verbal, and mental abuse for most of her married life. Dad wasn't around much but when he was it seems it was typically to inflict pain and damage. Although a talented mason, his talent was overshadowed by his addiction to alcohol. In my large family of eleven, I was the middle child. This sometimes made me feel sheltered; regrettably, the older kids would get the abuse from dad and the younger ones would typically get preferential treatment. I felt sandwiched between the bunch, and I made little attempts to get noticed.

My father was not the loving dad that I heard other girls talk about. I didn't get words of encouragement, hugs, or kisses. But I do remember the few times he seemed somewhat interested in his kids. One time was on a hot summer day. Dad was at the beginning stages of one of his drinking binges and appeared to be in a good mood. He took a few of us kids and cousins to a nearby lake; I couldn't have been more than twelve years old and it was a big treat anytime Dad took us anywhere, not for lack of time, but more so for lack of money and lack of interest on his part. He sat under a shady tree by the edge of the water as he watched us play. The summers were dry and scorching hot, and the cool water was a welcome relief.

After playing in the water for a while, my sister Lulu started struggling and yelling for help, desperately trying to keep her head above water. I reached out to grab her hand. I felt my feet get trapped in the sticky mud and I found myself going underwater also. When I finally got a hold of her, I realized that she was pulling me towards her. I was finally able to get my footing and I pulled her into shallower water. She was coughing and crying and I noticed Dad standing at the edge of the water with the legs of his pants rolled up to his knees, looking in our direction as if ready to jump in and rescue us. It was one of the few joyous occasions I recall from my childhood with my father; no,

we didn't get the hugs and loving words that you would expect a father to say after witnessing the danger that his daughters had struggled through…but it was a good feeling to know that he was ready to jump in and save us. In his own way he did love us, I suppose—in his own way.

As we grew older, it was interesting to see the stark differences in the life choices my siblings and I made. Even though we grew up in the same environment, with the same parents, some of us made less then productive lifestyle choices; choices that would later influence and affect the next generation of kids. However, I am a firm believer that in the end, in the final moments that test our character, we are each responsible for our own decisions and actions, regardless of our extenuating circumstances or influencing factors.

Like the rest of us, Sergio was not perfect and had some struggles he was working on; he too fell short in his walk with the Lord from time to time. I remember sometime during the last year of his life— he was an adult by then—he accompanied us to church on a Wednesday evening. He seemed uncomfortable, so I asked him what was wrong. "I feel bad, I feel ashamed to come back and face the people that helped me, when I have fallen short of God's expectations," he explained. I was grieved to hear the burden in his heart and I told him, "Don't let Satan deceive you from ever coming back to God; it is Satan that is trying to condemn you in an effort to destroy you. Do not let that happen because God loves you and always wants you to come to Him." I told him that feeling convicted was a good thing because it means that we feel ashamed of our sin and that we are uncomfortable with our actions. I told him that only through conviction, with a true spirit of contrition can forgiveness be granted by God; only then can a change of heart take place so that our life may be transformed. I assured him that it is those individuals that do not feel shame or remorse that should be concerned because that person does not care or is not convicted of sin, and therefore unable to obtain forgiveness. I urged him not to let sin permeate into other areas of his life and not to let Satan keep him from the glory of God, to learn from those sins and mistakes, and grow in his character with God's grace. I asked him not to give up on God because God was not going to give up on him; not now, not ever.

I patted his shoulder and told him the story of Danny, a youth pastor. I talked of the horrible life that young man had lived and how hard he worked to turn his life around and of the consequences he faced in doing so.

Sergio met that young pastor that night and, as it turned out, that pastor was one of the speakers at Sergio's funeral. No, Sergio was not perfect, who is? Neither parents nor children are perfect, and they don't come with a manual; but we must do the best we can every day so that in the end, our joys may be plenty and our regrets may be few.

Sergio was kind and gentle, and genuinely cared for those around him. He had strong convictions about family unity, about loyalty and friendship. He stood up for himself and spoke up for others when they needed him. He was a shield to many and a friend to most.

There was no shortage of love when it came to family ties. Sergio was close to several of our extended family members; the love they shared was deep and solid. I can recall countless illustrations that would help shed light into his character. However, the greatest testimony is not that Sergio was compassionate or that his relationships with those around him were based on love, respect, trust, and friendship, but that I believe the Lord has destined Sergio's death for a greater purpose...winning souls for God's glory.

At times, I think back to my pregnancy with Sergio and the blessing of holding him for the first time, feeling his warm body and instantly forgetting the labor pains that I endured during his birth. Then, remembering all the love and care that went into his upbringing, I realize that all the pain and struggles were more than compensated by the love and joy that he brought into our lives. His existence does not stop being real because he died but it brings greater meaning now because we've placed our faith and hope on the promise of eternity and salvation. We have lost our fear of death and we look forward to seeing him again in heaven, where it will be his turn to show us the ropes. We cling to the words of John in Revelation 21:4 (KJV) where he talks about the new heaven saying, *"And God shall wipe away all tears from their eyes; and there shall be no more death, neither sorrow, nor crying, neither shall there be any more pain: for the former things are passed away."*

A Mother's Closing Thought

There is no resentment in my heart for all the struggles
of your youth my child, but there is eternal love
and the memory of the joy you brought into my life.

Chapter Two

THE CALL

Like any mother, I had always worried about the safety of my children. My husband and I moved our family several times, in search of a safer place to raise them. At one point, we moved to Oregon seeking an opportunity for a better life.

Although we enjoyed living in Oregon, we were eventually forced to move back to California due to dismal employment opportunities. By that time, our two oldest boys were teenagers so we decided to settle in an area that was familiar to us. Our new home was close to my job and I was well aware of the surroundings. Displeased as I was with the dramatic down-sizing, the home was located in a decent, relatively safe area. That was our main concern, although we did have to make adjustments in order to accommodate a family of six.

Our kids grew up way too fast it seems; and years later, we found ourselves moving to a more comfortable home. We made sacrifices to be able to reside in a good area. We had a lovely home and felt very safe. We had great neighbors and our kids soon made friends, which added to the feeling of security. By this time, our two oldest had reached adulthood and were on their way to starting their own life.

We seemed to be leading a "normal" life; working hard, going to church, growing in our relationship with God, holding bible study at our home, spending time with the kids and their school projects, and making ends meet. Time with family was valuable; my husband and I had made it a point from the beginning of our marriage to treat each other and our kids with love and respect. We both come from large families and similar backgrounds; we had a lot in common, including the ideals we had for raising our children.

It was a sunny Sunday in 2004, when as I attended to routine family matters, I suddenly had an overwhelming need to talk to Sergio. He had been at our house the weekend before but he was staying at his grandmother's during the week. I made several attempts to reach him by phone though my mother told me that he was at the auto parts store getting tools to fix his car. I let the matter drop but later that evening when my husband, kids, and I were headed out to the market, I again felt the urge to talk to Sergio. I made another attempt and finally reached him.

I remember how good I felt when I heard his voice. I said, "Hey, how are you? You left without saying goodbye." He said he was sorry and asked how Dad was. I told him that his dad had four fractured discs in his back. I sensed a somber tone in Sergio's voice and asked if he was okay. Sergio began to weep; I remember wishing that I could hug him. It was not like him to cry; he was a strong young man and I thought that whatever was bothering him was much deeper than hearing the news of his father's condition.

I felt an overwhelming desire to share with him the word of God. I started by telling him that we had been praying for him. He replied as his voice began to break, "You'll never know how much your prayers mean to me." I was so comforted to hear that he appreciated those prayers. As parents, sometimes we feel like our kids don't always hear what we say to them, but it meant a lot to know that he was taking my prayers to heart. I was reminded of one of our pastor's messages that said, "When our kids are little, we talk to them about God; when our kids are older, we talk to God about our kids."

I told him that God loved him and was waiting for him. I wanted Sergio to know that God had a lot of joy and peace waiting for him; more joy than he could ever imagine. I told him that God has never left him and that God was knocking at his door, waiting for him to answer. But I never imagined that death was lurking just around the corner.

Towards the end of our conversation, his tone grew lighter, happier. I reminded him that I wanted the best for him. We talked about the test scores he'd received in his preliminary real estate exams, and I told him that I was proud of how well he had done. He and I had attended real estate school together. I asked him to come home the next day so we could prepare for the state exam. He agreed and said he'd be home after he got his car running.

During our conversation, I received a call from Lisa, one of my sisters calling about an issue with my son. In the past, she has been one of the siblings who went way off course and brought a lot of trouble into the family. This time she brought a really bad man into her life and it would bring dire consequences for all of us.

Lisa's given name is Refugio, meaning "refuge," but Cuca is the name that she grew up with and how my family refers to her. However, she never liked her name so she goes by the name of Lisa now; I will refer to her as Lisa throughout the remainder of this book.

My son was very concerned about the violence that Lisa's boyfriend, Bobby, was displaying towards her. Lisa seemed to take Bobby's side rather than think of her own safety or the safety of her children. I had talked to my kids on many occasions about the violence that my dad had inflicted on my mother, and I had shared with them how painful it was for me and my siblings to see him hurt her that way. Sergio was quite grieved by that because he loved his

grandma very much.

When I answered Lisa's call, I told her that I did not want to get into any drama and that I was on the other line in an important conversation with my son. I told her that I would return her call later. I went back to the call with Sergio, but I did not tell him who had just called. Now I know I should have let Sergio know that Lisa had called. It would have revealed the reason for his somber mood and may have prompted him to relay any concerns that he might have had.

Instead, I felt it was much more important for us to continue our conversation; the conversation I am now convinced was by divine appointment. Sergio and I agreed that we were a good team and we were looking forward to working together. By the end of the call, we were both feeling better. I told him, "I love you," and he reciprocated the sentiment by saying, "I love you too, Mom."

Later that Sunday, after the daily chores had been done and the pressing tasks completed, my husband and I prepared to have a relaxing evening at home with our two youngest kids. Then the phone rang and violently interrupted our plans, however.

I received a call from my baby sister, Veronica, it was 7:50 p.m., right after she had called 911. I could tell right away by the tone of her voice that something was seriously wrong. Her voice was shaky and broken, but she managed to utter a few words. She told me that Sergio had been stabbed in the heart and that he was unconscious and wasn't breathing. She said that the paramedics were working on him and she asked me to hurry over.

The pain that gripped my heart was immediate, and I began to panic. I asked who had done it and she told me it was Bobby. I immediately remembered that a week or so earlier Sergio had confronted Bobby for beating my sister Lisa. This attack by Bobby struck me as an act of revenge.

Shaken with fear, I told my husband what had just happened. He immediately gathered us together and began to pray. I was frustrated; I wanted to run to be by my son's side, and here my husband was, taking the time to pray. It takes a strong person to look to God for help before leaping into action. Action could be futile without the proper guidance from above.

Years later, I was provided with the following transcript of the call that my sister Veronica had placed to the 911 operator for assistance. She informed me that the call below was already the second call she made trying to get an ambulance to the scene. When I received the actual recording of the call, I was able to verify that the 911 operator did not call the ambulance until after a subsequent call was made from the police officer that arrived at the scene. It took over 15 minutes for an ambulance to arrive. In the call below, it appears the operator is more interested in finding out about the perpetrator than about sending medics, even after she is told that my son is unconscious and turning colors. But I digress.

Sunday at 19:41

OPERATOR: 911, what is your emergency?

CALLER: Um, somebody just got stabbed....and he's on the floor, um.

OPERATOR: Do you need paramedics?

CALLER: Yes

[Brother Raymond in the background yelling to the other perpetrators to leave …"leave already, leave…leave, leave."]

OPERATOR: Are they still…is the person that stabbed him is he still there?

CALLER: No, he left.

OPERATOR: Do you know who this was?

CALLER: Hello

OPERATOR: Do you know who the person was that stabbed him?

CALLER: Could you please just hurry up, cause he's on the floor unconscious.

OPERATOR: Okay, I need for you to stay on the line, okay? Where are you at right now?

[Caller to background: Yes, yes, that's what he stabbed him with, that's what he stabbed him with…..step on it, step on it]

[Unidentified-Male in background]

OPERATOR: Ma'am

[Background]

OPERATOR: Ma'am, where is the person that stabbed him?

CALLER: He left, he left.

[Background –Unintelligible]

OPERATOR: Who is the person that stabbed him or what did he look like and what was he wearing?

CALLER: Um, I don't know I just seen him, I just seen my nephew, cause it's my nephew...I just seen him on the floor. He's unconscious; can you please just hurry up?

OPERATOR: Okay, who is the person that stabbed him?

CALLER: I don't know that, I don't know that.

OPERATOR: Did you see the person—did you see him get stabbed?

CALLER: No, I just seen him on the floor with a stab wound on his chest.

[Background]

OPERATOR: You didn't see the per-

son that stabbed him?

CALLER: No, I didn't see, I just seen him on the floor, on the floor already.

OPERATOR: Okay, who was there that seen everything?

CALLER: Um, I don't know, I just got here.

OPERATOR: How old is your nephew?

CALLER: He's 21.

OPERATOR: Is he breathing right now?

CALLER: Um, [to someone in background: Is he breathing? Check if he's breathing].

CALLER to OPERATOR: He's breathing but he's unconscious. You need to hurry up 'cause he's purple and he's all these different colors.

OPERATOR: [To background: He's male Hispanic]

CALLER: [To background] They're coming, they're coming. I see them coming.

[Background-Unintelligible]

My family and I were not able to get to the scene on time, so we went straight to the hospital. As soon as we arrived, I went straight to the nurse and asked to see my son. We weren't allowed to see my son because the doctor was working on him. She showed us to a private room where we waited for the doctor to come speak to us. The room was very small and almost empty with just three or four chairs but I don't remember anything other than the plain, white walls.

I paced frantically, I cried, and I waited anxiously. My husband, daughter, and youngest son were with me in that awful room. My husband tried to calm me down and several times asked me to sit. But I couldn't stay still, I was so anxious and scared that I had to move, I had to walk, I had to do something. I tried to get the nurse to change her mind and let me in to see my son but she refused. It was simply torture having to wait for the doctor; it seemed like an eternity before he finally came in to talk to us. When he did, he first asked me to sit down and I reluctantly complied with his request. After a noticeable hesitation on the doctor's part, he finally said, "I am very sorry, we did all we could to save him…but he didn't make it." The doctor said he made the call to pronounce his death at 8:23 p.m.

I remember dropping back on the chair, feeling like the wind had just been knocked right out of me, like I had just entered into the most horrible nightmare; it was like an out-of-body experience, I honestly remember that the voices around me faded as I became engulfed with pain and I began to sob. I was in shock and denial; I had just spoken to my son an hour ago, this could not be happening. In that moment I did not think of those around me, not even my nine-year-old son Austin who was also in the room along with his older sis-

ter Jennie.

Instead of me being there for them, my young kids were there for me. My nine-year-old child, a very loving and caring little guy had brought his Bible with him. He opened it and read to me. I knew what he was doing and I was humbled by it. I heard him say the following words, *"Naked came I out of my mother's womb, and naked shall I return thither: the LORD gave, and the LORD hath taken away; blessed be the name of the LORD"* (Job 1:21, KJV). Now, I only remember hearing the part about giving and taking away. I could hear him reading, but it was like hearing the words through a tunnel, like a fading echo painfully piercing my heart.

I thought back to the prayers we immediately prayed after the phone call and all the way to the hospital. After getting the news from the doctor, I was left wondering if my prayers had not reached God in time. Did I not pray well enough or strong enough? Perhaps God

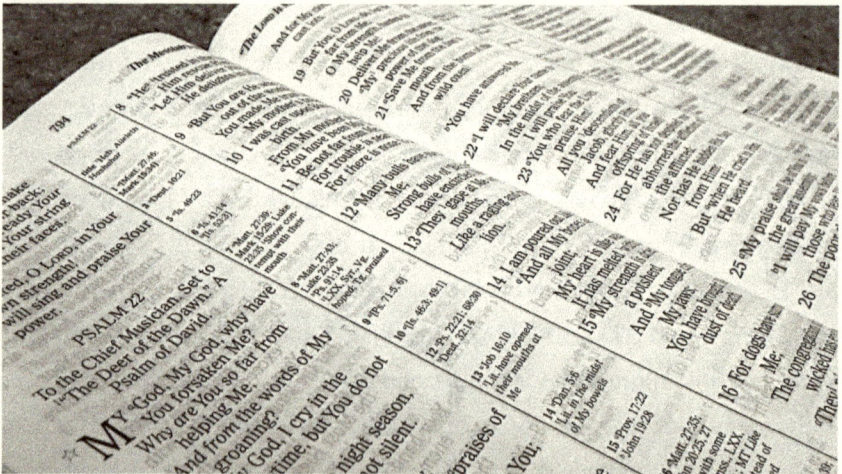

When the doctor told us Sergio was gone, I dropped in a chair—the wind knocked out of me. My nine-year-old opened his Bible and read out loud: *"Naked came I out of my mother's womb, and naked shall I return thither: the LORD gave, and the LORD hath taken away; blessed be the name of the LORD"* (Job 1:21, KJV).

had turned his head and allowed my son to die. Even though it certainly is not the same, I am reminded of the time when God turned from his own beloved son Jesus at the moment of his death. If God had allowed a sinless Jesus to die, surely he must have reasons for taking my son as well.

Leaving the emergency room a woman rushed over and asked me how my son was doing. I vaguely remembered talking to her on the way in to the emergency room. We had connected because both of our kids were being brought in by ambulance. I was suddenly brought back to reality when I heard her speak and I replied to her—in between sobs—that my son had just died. She looked at me in disbelief and offered her condolences and promised to pray for us. It was such a blow that I am still amazed I was able to stand despite the level of pain that overtook me. I didn't even think to ask about her son, I was so overwhelmed with my own pain.

As I focused on all that I was denied, the pain grew exponentially. I wasn't allowed to see my son before we left the hospital, although I pleaded with the doctor. I couldn't be there to help him; I couldn't kiss his wound and make it better like I had done so many times when he was a little boy, my little boy. My heart felt the pain that he must have felt in his heart with the stab wound. I felt the physical pain of that wound for a long, long time.

After a few minutes, my husband led us out of the emergency room and into the parking lot. I kept asking myself how in the world I would come up with the right words to tell the family. I was not yet ready to tell his older brother Andy that Sergio had just passed away, so I called my baby sister Veronica. I knew that she must have been anxious to hear that he was okay; that he had made it past the initial trauma and had survived.

I remember struggling to see the phone keys through my tears and when I finally connected with her, I could tell by her voice that she had been crying as well. She kept asking how he was, but I couldn't get the words out. I finally managed to say, "He died." She screamed and said, "No, don't tell me that, I don't want to hear that, Sandra." I heard her voice break as she tried to sound coherent between her cries; her voice was weak as she told our mom that Sergio had died, and then I heard the phone drop and only the sound of her sobs were audible. I waited for a few moments then I hung up the phone. I realized that Veronica had given up on that conversation... there was nothing left to say because I wouldn't bring back the hope that she had clung to for the last hour.

As we got into the car, I realized that I couldn't put it off any longer and that I had to call Andy and relay the devastating news. Andy had been out with his fiancée Rosemary. He called me as we were on our way home. His voice was shaking. Evidently he had talked to someone, but he didn't yet know the outcome. I was trying to avoid saying what the doctor had just told us but Andy repeatedly asked how his brother was. I mustered the courage to give him the devastating news—though I knew that the next words he would hear would cut him deeply.

Fighting through the immense lump in my throat had become painful. It was as if the inside of my throat was capturing all the pain and anger that was boiling up inside me and it was all bundling into a massive lump that would not let me speak. Somehow I managed to utter the news; the words reached his ears and now my pain became his own. He screamed and cussed as he tried to make sense of it; his pain was palpable and his anger quite justified; yet through his own devastation Andy found the compassion in his heart to tell me he loved me and that he'd wait for us to get to the crime scene.

My daughter Jennie, just a teenager at the time, was with us from the moment we got the phone call and was in the room when the doctor gave us the news. I remember how strong she seemed to me. I was amazed at her strength and composure through this horrific situation. She had always been close to her brothers and it seemed that she would have been more distraught over the loss of her brother. She was deeply distraught, but she was able to handle it much better than I did. I was comforted to know that indeed she had God's love and strength in her heart and I was certain that this is what was helping her get through this tragedy. I wish that I had taken some time to sit with her and her younger brother Austin to talk to them about their needs through that initial trauma.

As we approached my mother's house, the scene of the crime, I saw the police cars, the yellow crime-scene tape, and the witnesses scattered about the premises; it all seemed so surreal. I remember the lead detective was rude and condescending as he told me that he was not going to let anyone in. I asked him if he would allow me to be by my son's side at the hospital or at the morgue but he refused. He said that because it had been a homicide, they needed to protect the body from contamination and preserve it for evidence. In my head I understood his reasons but my heart's needs were stronger. The detective did not understand my need as a mother to be at my son's side; I was denied a mother's most basic and human need—to be by my child. Realizing that I would not be able to persuade him to grant me the approval to be with my son, I turned my focus on the place where we were—the crime scene.

I repeatedly asked the homicide detectives to let me in so I could see my mother but, again, they refused. The lead detective said, "You are not involved," in a very cold and detached demeanor. And although I understood what he was saying, I was also appalled by his approach and lack of compassion. I asked when I would be able to get in; they told me that it would be a long time because the witnesses were not cooperating and that the language barrier had become a problem.

I immediately offered to translate. I figured that if I translated for them, I'd be allowed to go inside. I was surprised when the lead detective's partner agreed and took me to the witnesses. My mother was the one that he needed me to translate for, so he walked me through the questions and I translated accordingly.

I was deeply saddened that the homicide had happened at mom's house; we grew up in that house and mom had worked tirelessly to provide a home for us. I felt for her, not only because of my son's death, but because my mom was very close to Sergio. As I followed the detective, I remembered Sergio as a child, running and playing in that same front yard. I recalled the countless times he visited his grandmother's house; considered it his second home. I cried at the feeling of helplessness; of not being able to change the situation or turn back time…just two hours would have been sufficient to prevent this nightmare from happening.

The detective also told me that my sister Lisa was not cooperating, saying that she didn't know anything about the killer. Lisa had been living with the killer for almost two years. I was so angry and hurt that I wanted to force her to cooperate, to force her to give the information that the officers needed. But as I approached the police car where she was being held, something inside told me to be calm. When I saw her she was sitting in the back of the patrol car and she looked up towards me but she would not look me in the eyes. I told her that

Sergio had died and she said that she knew. I asked her why she wasn't cooperating and told her, "There is nothing anyone could say or do to bring my son back, but we need you to help the detectives catch this man." She looked at me and said she didn't know anything. I saw a cold, calculated look on her face; not repentant or affected by my son's death, committed by the hands of her lover. I realized right then and there that she had turned her back on us and would protect that man no matter what. At that moment I felt she was a complete stranger. She would never again be connected to me or my family in any way; I would make sure of that. But at the same time I felt sorry for her, for what would become of her life.

Most of our family from both sides had gathered by then. I remember how painful it was when my oldest son arrived at the scene. He rushed to me and hugged me and began to sob. Here was this tall, strong young man falling apart in my arms; I felt weak at his pain. I had no words to comfort him as I was just as torn and broken as he. I couldn't offer any explanation or consolation for the loss of his brother or for this senseless act of cowardice.

As a parent of four children, I often wonder how God makes it possible for us to love our kids so much. I mean, when I had my first-born son, I loved him completely and wholeheartedly. I couldn't understand how a parent's love could expand to include more children. Amazingly, at the birth of each of our other children, I learned that God, in His perfection, somehow makes it possible for us to love each of our kids equally and wholeheartedly, but not separately. We love each of them 100% and yet we don't split that percentage by the number of kids…it's always 100%—and when one of them dies, likewise, it feels like your entire heart is taken, not just a respective percentage.

Our family offered us their support. We wept together and hugged each other. I remember sitting on the lawn, my knees folded into my chest, my head down, and my body curled up like a child—feeling so incredibly helpless, as I sobbed. My cousin's wife, Dolores sat by me and hugged me as I cried. I remember telling her that I felt like a bad mother for not being able to protect him. She replied that we can only do our best and there was nothing we could've done. I felt no comfort by her words but I knew they were true and I appreciated her sincere efforts to console me. I did feel we had always done our best to keep our kids safe—but somehow I came up short.

I knew that my husband and I had sacrificed for our children but this made me question my competence as a parent. What does this life really mean anyway, what is this all about and why work so hard to lead a good life and teach your kids well if someone will one day take it upon themselves to take their life…just like that, without a second thought.

My husband decided that we should go home as there was really nothing left for us to do. By that time it was already well past midnight. Arriving at our home was another painful reminder that our son would no longer be with us, that he would never again walk through that door and sleep in our home or spend time with us. My mother-in-law offered to accompany us and I was grateful for that because she was able to tend to the younger kids as I was certainly in no condition to care for them. I didn't even know if I was going to make it until morning myself with the intensity of the grief I was experiencing.

Needless to say, neither my husband nor I slept at all that night. I had lain awake thinking of the years that I was blessed to have had my son with us; I was never more aware of how fragile life is and how fast our kids grow up as I was that night. I ached to hold my son and longed to see him again. I desperately tried to think of how I could find a way to see him again, even knowing that his body was just a shell and that he wasn't there anymore, I needed to say goodbye. I felt cheated for the years I would never spend with him, and I felt guilty that he died before I did…that is not the way it's supposed to happen, that is not the normal progression of life. Parents aren't meant to out-live their children. I cried to the point where I could not think clearly, I kept thinking that at some point, the tears would have to stop flow-ing and that my body would eventually take a break, if only to prepare itself for the next 24 hours. I was terrified to think of how much deeper the grief would get, not knowing how I would react if I would have the opportunity to see my son's lifeless body, or how my heart would survive the anguish and torment of not knowing what was coming next and what we would be forced to confront. I prayed and reached out to God for mercy, for His love and grace to fill us during this chaos. I leaned on Him for guidance and wisdom, I couldn't do it on my own…my mind was much too clouded to make any rational decisions. I needed my heavenly Father to hold me and carry me through this nightmare.

A Father's Closing Thought

"I always looked out for my in-laws and their children;
but it seems that not all of them looked out for mine."

Chapter Three

THE MORGUE

Morning finally arrived after what seemed like an eternity. I just wanted to wake up from this nightmare and go see my son, alive and well. Facing reality, I forced myself out of bed to face a daunting day. I called several people trying to find a way to get to my son. I called my good friend Traci, and she immediately came to be by our side. She asked if there was something she could do for me and I told her that all I wanted was to see my son Sergio.

Traci made some phone calls and before I knew it, she had found a way to get us in. She very graciously offered to go with us, and I accepted. I was not in the proper state of mind to confront such a moment on my own, and my husband was not in the necessary physical condition considering his back injury, so he decided to wait outside the room at the morgue. As much as I wanted to see my son, I was deeply afraid that I would not be able to survive that moment, yet I was determined that nothing would keep me from being by his side.

This is by far a parent's worst nightmare. I never imagined I would ever have to face a moment like that. Words cannot describe the level of pain and helplessness that I experienced when I walked into the morgue and found my son laying there, lifeless. I kept looking for signs of breathing; I stared at his chest just hoping to see it rise, proving that this was all just a big cruel mistake or a stupid prank.

But I soon realized that my wishful and desperate attempts to escape reality were futile and that I had better come to terms with this

horrific reality because I did not have the power to change any of it.
He had some tubes in his mouth and it really hurt to see that. I wished
I could've taken them out so he would be comfortable. I wanted to
mother him and make it better for him. I vividly remember that even
then I thought that he was beautiful, strong, tall, and kind; to me he
was perfect, despite the signs of death. He looked as though he was
just sleeping. I noticed his freshly cut hair and how handsome he
looked. The only noticeable sign that he was dead was the dark red
color of his ears; I ached at the sight.

I wanted to die; more than that—I needed to die—it would be the
only way to stop the bleeding in my heart. I prayed to the Lord to take
me and let him live. After all, he deserved life much more than I. He
had his whole life ahead of him with dreams yet to fulfill. Homicide
case protocol and the preservation of evidence dictated that I only
view him through a glass wall…I was denied the right to hold my son
one last time. The shock and pain overwhelmed me and I became
silent for a few minutes, as if I had stopped breathing to mimic his
state.

My mind flashed to the memory of Sergio at the hospital at the
age of twelve when he had been sick with a high fever. His dad had
noticed his fever during the day while I was at work. My husband
called and told me that he had taken Sergio to the hospital because of
the fever and signs of dehydration. At the hospital, he was admitted
for observation. During that time, Sergio got progressively worse and
suffered a seizure. I had arrived at the hospital by then and I witnessed
the seizure, which made me panic. I called family and they arrived
soon after. Sergio fell into a coma and the doctors could not figure out
what the cause of the illness was, other than a possible viral infection
of some sort.

We all tried to wake Sergio from that coma. At one point, my husband told Sergio that he would take him fishing as soon as he woke up, so he needed to hurry up. This was a very scary time for us; we knew that the longer he stayed in that coma, the more dismal the situation would become. Through the night...just out of the blue, as my husband and I kept trying to wake him, he opened his eyes and said, "Hi." I began to cry profusely out of relief and had to step out of the room so as not to scare him. Later, on the ride home once he was released, he said to me, "Mom, why did you guys keep telling me to wake up?" His question surprised me; I thought that his state of unconsciousness prevented him from hearing us. I responding by asking him, "You could hear us?" To which he replied, "Yes, of course, I could hear everything." Curiously, I asked him why he would not wake up. He leaned on me as he softly said, "I was just too tired mom, and I wanted to sleep."

Those words now make me wonder if he can still hear me and sometimes I'd choose to think that he is just very tired and sleeping. He always hated it when we would wake him up early; he was definitely not a morning person and his sister and I knew that perfectly well. So I'll let him sleep and rest—rest my sweet. Other times I'll say to him from time to time, "Wake up sleepy head; wake up and let's go fishing." My thoughts reach out in an effort to reach him as I whisper, "Wake up and talk to me for a bit and let me know that you can hear me, that you will always hear me."

I was brought back to reality as I heard Traci call out to me repeatedly; I was saddened to realize the magnitude of that moment; standing in that room, experiencing such a painful episode that I knew I would never be able to erase from my mind or my heart.

I am eternally grateful to my friend Traci for making that visit

happen and for being there for me. If it had not been for her, I would not have been able to see my son before we buried him. Extenuating circumstances forced us to have a closed casket funeral. I feel I was robbed of the opportunity to hug and kiss him before he left us forever. I never got the chance to whisper in his ear the words, "I love you," like I did so regularly with all my kids. I whisper it now every time I visit his grave.

Once home, family and friends were there to comfort us…and they most certainly did. However, in the midst of all those people, I felt utterly alone; each one of us was steeped in our own pain and sorrow. Ever so grateful for those who covered us in love and prayers, I knew they all cared, but I also knew that they couldn't possibly understand the level of sorrow that I was facing.

I spoke to my sister Veronica the day after the homicide and she told me that she was there when Sergio was talking to me over the phone and she told me that she noticed that he was happier after our conversation. She said he told her that he was looking forward to coming home the next day.

Veronica shared with me the painful details of what had transpired during the altercation. Veronica further shared with me that after the fight, Sergio had shown her his wound and she saw the knife still inserted into his body. She explained that he pulled the knife out and immediately collapsed. His lungs were desperately struggling for air as his skin began to turn pale. She delicately told me before he died his last words were: "It hurts, it really hurts"—words that live on to haunt and torment me to this day. My other sister Lisa, the woman who babysat him as a child, whom I trusted completely, looked down at my son and said, "That's what you get." Rather than having compassion for her own flesh and blood, she sided with a killer.

Sometimes I wonder if my son heard her say those words and if so, did he regret defending his aunt against this man? I ask myself how he would have felt... betrayed?

I had the overpowering need to know everything; it was as if I wanted to immerse myself in the scene, to know the whole truth—if only I could've been there—in a strange effort to feel closer to my son. I was obsessed with discovering every detail but at the same time, some of the most painful details were those that were relevant to his body and his life.

It pains me to think that he pulled the knife out of his chest himself and that he turned purple while gasping for air. Not to mention the pain I felt on learning that he had turned cold and his eyes had rolled back and that my brother's wife Julie is the one that closed his eyes when she realized that he had died. Hearing that the doctors had done emergency surgery when he arrived at the ER, and in fact tried to revive him by taking his heart out of his chest and pumping it by hand trying to revive him…these were all extremely painful words to hear and accept.

A stab in the heart caused him to collapse; his life slowly drained from him as he frantically gasped for air. Yes, his life was taken, but the love we shared remains. There is such a special bond between a parent and child that even death cannot break. The grief is so intense and debilitating because the love is so deep…the connection is eternal.

Someone hurt my child, took it upon himself to end his precious life. I often wonder if the killer ever thinks about what he did, or was this just another strike; another point in his book of violent deeds. I ask myself if that man's holidays are joyous, or have they ever been overshadowed by the fact that he killed another human being, that he

robbed a family of such special moments and a life full of potential. I wonder if the killer has ever lost a night's sleep over what he did; if the gravity and measure of his actions ever cause him pain…does it ever cross his mind? Does he look at himself in the mirror and like what he sees, or does he ever look at his hands and sees my son's blood reflected upon them? I'm torn between hoping that this man one day has children of his own so he can ponder the possibility of losing one of them, and torn by hoping that he never feels the joy of the love of a child. I may never know, but this I do know, he killed my son's body, but he could never kill his spirit.

The killer's family somehow managed to get a copy of my son's autopsy report at least a week before we were able to receive our copy. I am not sure how they finagled this or what strings they pulled in order to do this. The killer's sister called me the day she received the report. She wanted to make sure I knew that they had "connections;" I was overcome with anger. A week later when I finally received the report, I was distraught; it was a painful reminder of the finality of Sergio's death…as if I needed a reminder.

The report was horrific to read; to see how invasive and intrusive that exam had been. I felt appalled at this because this was my child, my son, and he was exposed for the whole world to see, "But he was the victim!" I screamed inside. I felt for him and it was as if he'd been victimized all over again. In my mind I understood the process, but in my heart was the resentment that only a parent can feel when his or her child is assaulted. In a particular section of the report, I read that the state of his teeth were "in good condition." Tears flowed as I recalled the years of braces and the countless times I nagged Sergio to brush his teeth and put his retainer on…ugh, he hated that thing! "In good condition," indeed! Those teeth gave him such a beautiful smile, a smile that melted hearts. The tears continued to flow as I remembered that after Sergio died, his friend returned his belongings to me, including his toothbrush.

Then I read something that is not easy to talk about, something still hard for me to understand and accept. I was distraught to read information that was less than favorable to Sergio, which the defense capitalized on. I questioned whether I should even include this information here, and I came to the conclusion that I need to keep it real, to be as honest and transparent as possible in order to portray an accurate representation of the case, the entire case. It was extremely painful to learn that the toxicology report showed that Sergio had a low level of drugs in his system. I felt broken by this revelation and I was confused. I felt like a failure, wondering why my child would resort to such a thing. "Why would he do that?" I asked myself. He knew how we felt about drugs, and we worked so hard to teach all of our children right from wrong. In fact, when Sergio was twelve years old he was part of a drug prevention program where he was forced to make some tough decisions with his school peers and his decisions earned him an award.

Needless to say, the killer and his collaborators used this information to portray him as a monster but everyone that Sergio knew and all those around him know differently. Like I said, Sergio was not perfect and I was concerned this information would reflect negatively on him. Nonetheless, I trust this information will help others and, if nothing else, shows that when we die, all is revealed and may be used against us. Still, Sergio did not initiate the altercation that night, and he certainly did not deserve to be ambushed and stabbed to death.

It wasn't until just recently that my daughter brought something to my attention that made me wish I had thought about during the

trial. When Jennie and I were discussing this information for the book and when I explained to her that Chela, the killer's sister, had somehow been able to get a copy of the autopsy report before we were allowed to, Jennie said to me, "Mom, if those people had these kind of inside connections, then perhaps they were able to have the toxicology report altered." I felt a sick feeling in my stomach because she had a valid point. I know it may seem that I am simply in denial about this, but after everything we witnessed, I am keenly aware that anything is possible.

Finally, I get to the part of the autopsy report that talks about the fatal wound, the precise and medical terms used to describe what in layman's terms we know as a stab in the heart. Ironically, it would have to be his heart that would be pierced. The killer would deliberately choose to stab him in the heart, to make Sergio's heart stop beating. After all, it was Sergio's greatest attribute; his heart, kindness, love, selflessness—he gave love so freely and never expecting anything in return. A heart so compassionate that resentment had no place in it and could not harbor hate or malice…it would have to be his heart. In contrast, the killer was filled with hate. He is a degenerate whose life is toxic to everyone around him. He decayed to the point of becoming capable of taking another person's life and took it upon himself to eliminate anyone that would challenge him or confront him.

My heart has been ripped right out of my chest and left open to shrivel and die slowly; exposed for all to see, vulnerable to the elements that can continually tear away and shake me to the core, to the point of self-destruction if I'd let it. Elements that may or may not be visible or tangible but can become prey to a wounded spirit and fragile state of mind. It affected every aspect of my life and the life of my

AUTOPSY

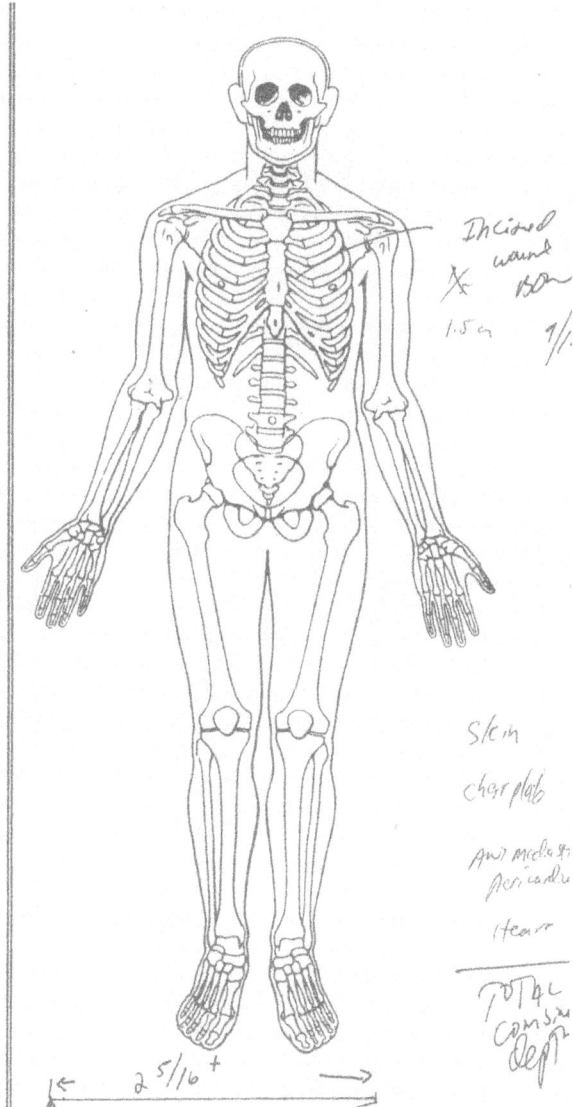

family, even in areas that we desperately tried to protect. Our view of the world became tainted by the grim shades we were now seeing the world through, the darkness of evil that tears away at the basic joys of life, the simplest of things that somehow become unbearable, and even the big important things now have become bitter-sweet.

A Father's Closing Thought

"In my deepest pain, I wanted to honor God—even in my grief—I wanted to bring it all back to Him, to reach out to Him because I felt I was nothing."

Chapter Four

THE FUNERAL

Ten agonizing days passed before our son's body was released. His death was ruled a homicide and required a thorough investigation. Adding to our stress, I felt the need to arrange the funeral as soon as possible since some of our family members had traveled a long distance to pay their respects. Planning a funeral in the midst of our grief was a daunting task. I wanted everything to be perfect; after all, I was a mother taking care of my precious son's final needs.

Looking back, I thank God for the delay caused by the investigation. The extra days provided time for me to pray about two of my most immediate concerns. The first and most important was my son's salvation. As a Christian, your hope of salvation is what makes the trials in this life bearable. When Sergio died, I was tormented by the thought that he may not have accepted Jesus as his Lord and Savior.

We raised our son as a Christian, but we also recognized that choosing Christ was a personal decision that Sergio needed to make on his own. A couple of days passed and I remember calling one of our pastors and relaying my concerns. Pastor Didel and his wife Maria came to visit with us the following Wednesday. I clearly remember sitting with them in the privacy of our bedroom and his wife asking me when I last spoke to Sergio. I explained that I had talked to him about an hour before he was killed.

I continued telling Maria that I had shared with Sergio that our bible study group had prayed for him. I shared with Maria that he had left to his grandmother's house the week before and that I had asked him to come home the next day. I spoke about our final phone conversation and the words I shared with Sergio, which I felt in my heart God wanted him to hear. Words such as: God loves you and is waiting for you. He is knocking at your door but you need to reach out to him and accept His invitation. I told her that Sergio acknowledged my words and agreed to come home the next day and join us in bible study; it was then that I noticed Maria's face change as she gently smiled. I paused as she said, "Do you hear what you're saying? That's your confirmation right there, that he is saved." I felt an amazing peace because I realized that the phone call and conversation I had shared with him was not by chance, it was by divine appointment; the need I had to speak with him wasn't just for me; it was God's message that needed to reach him before he died.

God, in his infinite wisdom, found the perfect way to communicate to Sergio the words that he needed to hear before he was called home...to his eternal home. I went to my room and opened my daily devotional book from Charles Spurgeon and I opened it to the day Sergio died, April 25th. I was amazed at what I found written for that evening, and I cried as I read the following because it was almost the same as the words I spoke to Sergio in our last conversation:

> *"Open the door, beloved, and He will come*
> *into your souls. He has long been knocking,*
> *and all with this object, that He may sup*
> *with you, and you with Him. He sups with*
> *you because you find the house or the heart,*
> *and you with Him because He brings the pro-*
> *vision. He could not sup with you if it were*
> *not in your heart, you finding the house; nor*

could you sup with Him, for you have a bare
cupboard, if He did not bring provision with
Him. Fling wide, then, the portals of your
soul. He will come with that love which you
long to feel; He will come with that joy into
which you cannot work your poor depressed
spirit; He will bring the peace which now you
have not; He will come with His flagons of
wine and sweet apples of love, and cheer you
till you have no other sickness but that of
'love o'erpowering, love divine.' Only open the
door to Him, drive out His enemies, give
Him the keys of your heart, and He will
dwell there forever. Oh, wondrous love, that
brings such a guest to dwell in such a heart!

I feel very blessed and honored to have been the vessel that God chose to let Sergio know how much He loved him. Many times I've wondered what that encounter must've been like, when Sergio came into the presence of the Lord; what, if anything, was said by Sergio. I was told days later that Sergio had been somber the day he was killed, he'd been saddened over a petty issue that ensued with my sister Lisa and her lover, the same one that would later take Sergio's life. I was told that Sergio had felt such a heavy heart over the trivial issue that caused the altercation.

And so realizing that the Lord had a purpose for that call gave me hope, the hope I needed to get through those painful moments and through the funeral. I began to pray for guidance. I asked God if there was something that He needed me to do with all of this, and as painful as this situation was, I surrendered my will to God. I prayed and meditated on the notion of being used by God for His glory.

Thoughts entered my mind about writing a eulogy. I felt the responsibility to address friends and family at the funeral service and talk about the obligation that God places on us to hold our kids accountable and teach them about God while also providing love and encouragement. However, I didn't believe that I would have enough composure to carry myself through it. My husband and I also wanted to defuse the anger that was building around us. I felt the burden to address the crowd to share God's love, peace, and purpose. The delayed funeral gave me time to think and pray about all of that. I believe that focusing on the funeral arrangements kept me from going insane with the reality of what had been done to my son, a cruel betrayal and brutal homicide.

I channeled my energy, pain and anger on those items as well as tried to be there for our other kids, although I am certain that I must not have done as well as I should have. I was very thankful for family members that periodically offered to keep the kids; it was a relief to know that we had people around us we could trust.

This was particularly meaningful because I had become very nervous that something might happen to my other children. I had a heightened sense of fear that the killer or his minions would hurt my other kids as well.

During the days that followed I was in shock. It was as if I existed in a haze. Time slowed to a halt, yet I barely remember exactly what transpired. The kindness we experienced from so many people was heart-warming and very comforting. It still amazes me that people from all walks of life including friends, family, and people we didn't even know, selflessly offered their help and support. We are forever grateful to those that were there for us when we needed them most.

I remember acts of kindness like the time that my cousins and uncle drove for hours from Sacramento to be with us. Just a few short months prior, my husband and I had been at their mother's funeral and now, it seemed, it was our turn. When they arrived at our house, my cousin Jesse offered to mow our lawn. I remember that I was opposed to this, but when my cousin learned that my husband had recently been injured, he felt the need to help. I told Jesse that it wasn't necessary, but he replied that this was his way of serving the Lord. I simply could not object. I was humbled and made aware that I had no right to hinder whatever blessings God had in store for this man for his good heart.

A couple of days later, my sisters Lety and Veronica, as well as my cousin's wife, Dolores, went with my husband and I to select the casket; their presence helped us bear that painful experience. They were also there for me when I had to endure the torture of having to select the outfit that my son would wear for his funeral.

Our family and friends helped financially as well, and brought food over for everyone; I simply didn't think about eating, and I certainly didn't think about cooking. I'm grateful to my cousin Brenda who, after driving a long distance, still had the energy and desire to help around the house. I can't begin to tell you how broken I was and how these acts of kindness blessed and lifted my spirits.

We are truly blessed to have such a large and loving family. My husband and I went to a few cemeteries trying to find the best plot for Sergio, as if there was such a place. I know that my husband was exhausted from the debilitating pain of his injured back, which must have made this nightmare even worse. Sitting in the office of one of the funeral homes, I remember asking my husband his thoughts for the funeral service options that were offered. The broken man sitting

before me replied, "Whatever you prefer, I just want to get it over with." Not realizing that his choice of words were hurtful, I began to cry and said, "I don't want to get this over with, I feel like once this is all over he will be gone forever and I am not ready to let him go yet." I understood what he meant but in my desperation, I was trying to hold on to Sergio longer than humanly possible.

I came to know of the strength and resiliency of my children, of their love and commitment to our family unit. In my heart I hold a special place for a moment I shared with my daughter, Jennie. I don't remember how it came to be that she and I were alone with as many people as were at my home that day, but at this particular moment, we were alone together in my bedroom. I realized that she, too, was going through a horrible ordeal.

She had always been very close to her siblings and I know this must have been excruciating for her, although she never seemed to show how destroyed she was. I asked how she was, and she said she was okay. I touched her long, silky hair and told her that it was okay to cry. She told me that Sergio had always taught her to be strong, both with his words and with his actions. We shared a very special moment together in the middle of this nightmare and I wished I could have somehow spared her from her pain.

Oddly, strangers were not strangers in the midst of this tragedy. I marveled at the outpouring of generosity shown to us by so many, even those we had never met before. When someone is killed, it affects not just a family, but an entire community, even entire generations. I was touched to see Sergio's friends come and offer their heartfelt condolences. They were mourning the loss of a great friend and confidante; many even considered him a brother. Their loss was significant as well.

On one occasion, I was sitting in the family room surrounded by my brothers and sisters, and my mom. I remember feeling so desperately sad and painfully aware of the reality of losing a child when I realized that my mom had experienced that same pain. I turned to her and told her, as I struggled through my tears that I now realized what she must have suffered when she lost her 29 year-old son, Martin. I was deeply amazed to hear her reply as she choked on her words, "Yes, but as painful as that was, Sergio's death is even more devastating."

The sound of those words echoed in my mind and I fell apart. Martin had epilepsy and had died tragically. He had a seizure while in the shower and somehow a washcloth clogged the drain and he drowned. That too, was a tragic death that happened at my mother's house and it impacted all of us deeply. Martin was a very special man who sacrificed a lot to help provide for the family.

We were very poor when we lived in Mexico; in fact, our family shared only one bedroom. I remember the floor was just the soil and the entire house was inches off the foundation which left room for critters and a chilly draft during the winter; but I also remember we were happy, at least us kids that were oblivious to the burdens of life. I loved being part of a large family because even if you got upset with one of your siblings, there were always more to play with. Mom, Martin, and my oldest sister Maria worked very hard to help provide for our large family, which at the end totaled eleven plus mom and dad.

I am certain that life was not fun for them, and my childhood happiness probably felt different to them as they were the ones who carried the burden. One of the most special memories I have of Martin is from when I was about four years old. It was Christmas morning

and Martin had been working through the night. It seemed that while everyone else was celebrating Christmas, we were struggling to just have enough to eat.

I remember my brother came home that cold Christmas morning and brought with him the most beautiful little Christmas tree; and if I remember correctly, it had lights as well. The tree couldn't have been taller than two feet, but to us, it was the most beautiful tree in the world. The sad thing is that when dad got home and saw the tree, he threw it out in one of his rants, I was heartbroken. Martin and Maria helped my mother for years and I never heard them complain. They sacrificed a lot and I thank them from the bottom of my heart. I know my mother must have felt lost without him. I was close to him and his death was a tremendous loss for me as well. I remember the kind advice he gave me when I started dating the young man that would eventually become my husband.

I always felt loved by Martin; I felt protected and guided by the way he led his own life. I recall a time when I was going to run away from home. Again, I could not have been more than four years old but I was determined to leave. I can't remember what I was upset about, but there I was, packing my most prized possessions- my dolly and my jump rope. I started to head out the house and onto the hill that was behind our home. Martin and Mom saw me and I remember they chuckled as they saw me make my way up the hill. Mom asked me "Where are you going, Sandra?" I told her that I was running away, I noticed that Martin was holding back his laughter as Mom continued her questioning, "Well, where are you going?" At the casual tone of her voice, I became indignant because it seemed like they didn't believe me. She had nine kids at the time so she probably had seen this stunt before. Looking back at it now, I am certain this must have seemed like the many times my own children pulled their own stunts on me, and I laughed at some of the things they do because they are so cute and innocent. I was very determined to leave and I told mom that I was running away to grandma's house; now keep in mind that I had absolutely no idea where grandma lived, but I was leaving nonetheless. At this point Martin could hold his laughter no longer and he said, "Look, you can leave if you don't want to live here with us anymore, we won't hold you against your will," he seemed sincere so I listened intently as he continued "but remember, it gets really cold at night and it gets very dark out there. I know how much you hate that but I assure you that is the least of your concerns," he affirmed. Hearing this made me ponder my situation and I felt I could negotiate a deal but before I could speak he said "here, take my sling shot and take this ammo, you will need it to fight off the wolves and the rats." I began to cry, and he began to laugh…he knew how much I hated rats! He came and picked me up, hugged and kissed me. Mom just smiled as she shook her head and went back to do laundry. Needless to say, I never pulled that one again.

Martin was very close to Sergio Jr. and loved him dearly, so when my brother died, I believe my mother loved Sergio that much more to make up for the loss. I know that Sergio always held a special place in my mother's heart after my brother's death. I understand that too, because after Sergio died I found myself clinging to anything that would remind me of him. I often found myself seeing Sergio in others with similar features and now—more and more—I see a lot of Sergio in my youngest son Austin.

During the days leading up to the funeral I was determined to write a message for the eulogy not knowing if I would have the strength to deliver it myself or not. I just needed his funeral to have great significance and be a true representation of God's presence in our lives. I asked my cousin Jesse to say the eulogy in case I was not able to, and if I was, to interpret in Spanish; he kindly agreed.

We held the funeral at our home church, Calvary Chapel in Diamond Bar, and although we were unable to have our pastor, Raul Ries, perform the service, having the funeral there was comforting because we had been members of the church for over fifteen years. Pastor Raul did take the time to meet with my husband and me at a later time to counsel with us and pray with us during our mourning period. We truly appreciate that despite the fact Pastor Raul has a con-gregation of about 15,000; he cared enough to pray with us during our time of need. It was this type of leadership that brought us to the church to begin with. It was also the place where I volunteered to translate the women's studies and a book for Pastor Raul. Having our son's funeral there was a tremendous blessing for us.

Up until the moment I was called up to say the eulogy, I was pray-ing for strength and peace to say what God would have me say, in this, the most horrible time of my life. I took a deep breath and suddenly, I felt the most amazing peace. It was a supernatural peace and I knew it could only come from God. I gave the eulogy without losing it. At that moment I knew that the Lord had a purpose for it all...even if I didn't understand it then.

In my message, I talked about parenting God's way; that we are to teach our children about God, love them, hold them accountable, and talk to them regularly about their needs. I also said that even though we had been going to church for a long time and that we had taught our children about the Lord, that it was in this moment that we had to prove to ourselves that we believe everything we had learned about God. This was our biggest trial and it was up to us, no matter how painful, to bring testimony and witness to the Lord. I talked about the last conversation I had with Sergio just prior to his death and about the honor it was for me to be the one that God used to deliver that message to him.

After the service, I was told that 19 people raised their hand to accept the Lord that day. Among them was my youngest brother Ramon, a young father who realized that he needed to change his own life for the sake of his son. Ramon wanted to give his son the same things that I fought so hard to give mine... a fighting chance at life; one without all the bad influences and toxic relationships that at one point began to lead Sergio astray. I was also told that many people were inspired by the peace found in that message, and it brought me comfort to know that God's word reached the hearts of others in the midst of all the chaos.

A young man that was also a church staff member beautifully sang one of the songs we chose for the funeral. He asked us which songs we wanted him to play and sing for us, I immediately thought of a song I'd heard long prior to my son's death, it was a song that made me cry when I heard it because it was profoundly sad and beautiful at the same time; it went perfectly with the theme we decided on for the funeral service. On the program cover was an image of Jesus hugging a young man at the divine moment they meet in Heaven. It reminded me of the Bible scripture in (2 Corinthians 5:8) *"We are confident, I say, and willing rather to be absent from the body, and to be present with the Lord."*

Similarly the following song speaks of that indescribably beautiful moment. The song is called "When God Ran" by Benny Hester, who very graciously allowed us to include his song lyrics in this book.

When God Ran - Recorded by: Benny Hester
Written by: Benny Hester & John Parenti

Almighty God
The Great I Am
Immovable Rock
Omnipotent powerful

Awesome Lord
Victorious Warrior
Commanding King of Kings
Mighty Conqueror

And the only time
The only time I ever saw Him run
Was when He ran to me
Took me in His arms, held my head to His chest
Said, "My son's come home again."
Lifted my face, wiped the tears from my eyes
With forgiveness in His voice
He said "Son, do you know I still love you?"

It caught me by surprise when God ran

The day I left home
I knew I'd broken His heart
I wondered then
If things could ever be the same

Then one night
I remembered His love for me
And down that dusty road
Ahead I could see

It's the only time
The only time I ever saw Him run

When He ran to me
Took me in His arms, held my head to His chest
Said, "My son's come home again."
Lifted my face, wiped the tears from my eyes
With forgiveness in His voice
He said, "Son, do you know I still love you?"
It caught me by surprise
It brought me to my knees
When God ran

I saw Him run to me
And then I ran to Him

Holy One, Righteous Judge
He turned my way
Now I know He's been waiting
For this day

And then He ran to me
Took me in His arms, held my head to His chest
Said, "My son's come home again"

Lifted my face, wiped the tears from my eyes
With forgiveness in His voice
I felt His love for me and then He

He said Son, He said Son, My Son
Do you know I still love you?
Oh He ran to me
When God ran

My son, Andy (left) was a pallbearer at his brother's funeral. I will never forget the look of ultimate sorrow on his face and on the faces of his sister, Jennie, and his brother, Austin.

My oldest son Andy, only a year older than Sergio, was one of the pallbearers; he and Sergio were very close. As everyone proceeded to walk out of the church, I saw on the faces of my other kids, Andy, Jennie and Austin, a look I will never forget. Reflected upon them was the raw pain of the trauma that had been violently thrown upon them. I vowed never to forget that look, the look of ultimate sorrow. Seeing my children suffer like that ripped away at my soul.

Closing Thought

"When we forget about them, that's when they are really gone."

Chapter Five

THE FUGITIVE

After the funeral, the focus turned to finding Bobby, the accused who was now a fugitive. Although it took a long time for the detectives to determine where the killer was, a lot of things happened in the interim. Shortly after the funeral, I made it a point to do whatever I could to help law enforcement, but also felt I should try to bring awareness to the community and seek their support. We did several press conferences and newspaper articles in efforts to expand the resources for broader coverage and hopefully faster results. But as soon as the news hit the streets, we began to get harassing phone calls at home from the killer's family members. This was certainly not the first time that those people were in trouble with the law; these are criminals that know how to work the system and are not afraid to hurt anyone that crosses their path. My niece had shacked up with the killer's nephew and my sister had shacked up with the killer, despite how much all our family objected to those relationships, these two did not heed our warnings.

I felt betrayed by both my niece, Monique, and certainly by my sister Lisa; not to mention by the killer who had forced his way into our family. A few years prior, Monique had been kicked out of her home and had nowhere to go. No one wanted to take her in because of her rebellious behavior. My husband and I offered her an opportunity for a fresh start. We had a very small house then, but we welcomed her into our home and she shared a room with my daughter. We registered her at our local school and provided for her as best we could. However, it soon became very clear why she was having so many problems at home; she quickly became rude and defiant. We struggled to correct her deceitful and manipulative behavior at our home and in school and after a short time, we realized that she was a bad influence on our daughter and we had no choice but to take her back to her mother's house. Several times we had given Monique the opportunity to rectify her behavior, but she made no attempts to change her ways. To this day we feel she never appreciated our efforts, but that is between her and God. We feel that we did what we thought was the right thing to do. We were saddened to hear of her association with the killer's family and hoped that as she grew older she could see the destructive path that lay ahead and that she would wise up…but that was not for us to decide. When we took her back to her mother's house we prayed that what we showed her would plant a seed in her heart that would someday sprout good things in her life and those around her. My heart breaks at the thought of what my sister Lulu has suffered over her daughter's actions. I know it must be devastating to know that your child is capable of causing such damage. It is like a double-edged sword for me when I think about my family members being involved in my son's death, and it pains me to know how much it has torn the family apart.

Layer after layer of sorrow was caused by my son's death. I agonize over the time I had to go to the social security office to close out his social security number because someone had stolen his birth certificate just a few days after he died. I still remember the lady's expression that attended to me that day at the social security office. She asked why I was closing Sergio's number, and as composed as I tried to be, I still fell apart as I explained that he had been killed; she felt my pain and she cried with me. I remember the heartache I felt when I received his death certificate and as I laid it beside his birth certificate. I felt such anguish and disgust at the thought of the cowardly killer who took my son's life.

It was eventually revealed that the killer had fled to Mexico. The detectives were tracking Lisa and the other crime contributors; they knew that one of them would lead to the killer. It was now January, over eight months since my son's brutal death. By this time, the detectives were working closely with the US fugitive task force and with the Mexican Federales on strategic surveillance operations.

Reading back through my journal, I found an entry dated January 10th, where I pray for the killer to be captured. A few days beforehand, my friend Mike had prayed with me over my grief and frustration concerning the evasive fugitive. Mike told me that he felt that the killer would be caught soon, "Before February 25th." So, in the journal entry I wrote a specific prayer for the killer to be captured before February 25.

On Sunday February 21, my prayer was answered. I received a call from the homicide detective telling me that the killer had been arrested the night before. It was an amazing answer to prayer, fulfilled before the date I had asked for. I was relieved that this killer was off the streets and hopeful that justice would soon be served. After ten excruciating months, the killer was finally arrested, and, as predicted, Lisa was right there with him. They were both apprehended and extradited the same night. I cannot begin to explain the feeling of relief I felt as I heard those words. I could finally rest, letting my relentless drive to find him subside. I took a deep sigh as I thanked God. I am certain that I must have been driving my husband crazy. At one point I had even asked my husband to drive me to Mexico so that we could

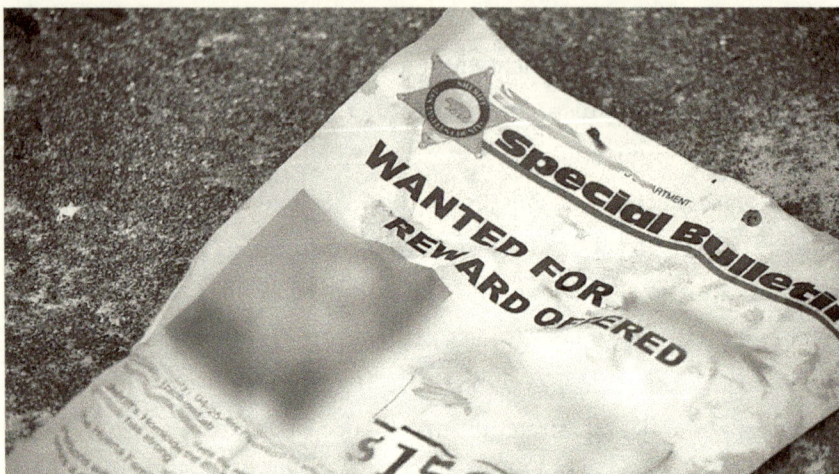

The killer had been on the run for ten excruciating months. At one point, I became so exasperated, I asked my husband to drive me to Mexico so we could hand out copies of the "Wanted" flyers to Border Patrol agents.

take the "Wanted" flyers to the border patrol agents.

The killer was not a stranger, this was not a random act of violence; with two other felony convictions he was indicted for first-degree murder and other counts of witness intimidation. If convicted, the killer would serve life on a mandatory three-strikes-law. I admit that I often wondered what would have happened if the killer had resisted the arresting officials. I asked the homicide detective, and he answered, "These killers are typically big cowards and they know when they are trapped, they know they can get killed if they put up a fight." He continued, "I heard that as the officials broke in and surprised them, the situation seemed quite pathetic to see the weak behavior of this idiot."

My husband and I became very concerned for the safety of our other kids. The killer's family made several harassing phone calls to us and left notes on the windows of our business. We struggled over the decision to move out of the area. Eventually, we lost our business. I couldn't focus on anything except finding the person that killed my son.

Those making threats are people without a moral compass, willing to do anything to get what they want. They wreak havoc, destroy lives, and taunt you in the process. In fact, my sister Lisa went as far as stealing from our own father. He became disabled and she offered to help him. It was eventually discovered that she took power-of-attorney over his matters and used it to wipe out his savings account. Any other references to her character would be pointless. It isn't that she wasn't loved, she was, very much so—and by all of us—but she chose a very different way of life and we had no say so in it.

I felt especially hurt by Lisa's actions. I had always thought that she and I were close. I had trusted her to babysit Sergio when he was a baby. She asked me to be her son's Godmother; but none of this mattered when she chose to side with Bobby.

Defending Lisa, two weeks prior to the homocide, was a huge factor in the altercation that resulted in Sergio's death. Sergio was saddened and distressed that he had to be the one to address this issue because nobody else would. I called Lisa the next day and offered to help her. I told her that she was not safe and offered to take her to church, to which she replied, "No thanks, I've tried the church thing but that didn't work for me." I later learned that this man had been beating her up for a while, but she did not want to call the police and she had no intention of leaving him. Based on Sergio's upbringing, and knowing how domestic violence had affected his grandmother, Sergio felt the responsibility to put a stop to the violence. My son was more concerned about his aunt's safety than his own, but in Bobby's world, there was a pecking order. He was certainly not going to let this

dressing down by a younger man go unpunished. Bobby's revenge was to ambush my son the gangster way – my son was outnumbered and they were armed during the altercation that led to Sergio's death. Nevertheless, I am reminded of the story of Joseph, as found in Genesis 37:18-20 (KJV)

> "*18And when they saw him afar off, even before he came near unto them, they conspired against him to slay him. 19 And they said one to another, Behold, this dreamer cometh.20 Come now therefore, and let us slay him, and cast him into some pit, and we will say, "Some evil beast hath devoured him: and we shall see what will become of his dreams."*

Yes, Joseph was betrayed by his own brothers. Yes, he suffered and endured great struggles, but God had great plans for him. And no matter how hard Satan worked to destroy Joseph, God worked that evil plot for good. We have to be willing to serve the Lord despite the pain. Even though Joseph was betrayed, attacked, and found himself in miserable circumstances, God did not leave him.

Closing Thought

"Should a man's entire life be defined by a single action, a specific moment in time? Perhaps, that is a fair price to pay for taking a human life."

Chapter Six

THE TRIAL

After many months of continuances and delay tactics on behalf of the defense, I was able to face the man that killed my son. It was incredibly painful to see the man that mercilessly took Sergio's life. At the preliminary trial, the prosecution was able to succeed in securing a murder trial. We spent many more months waiting for the actual trial as the defendant was stalling for time until he could retain a private attorney.

Seeing my sister Lisa at the trial was very painful. Part of me wanted to yell at her and shake some sense into her; while another part of me wanted her to come to me and tell me that she was sorry for everything that happened, for her part in it…part of me wished we could resolve that issue before the trial began. But alas, there was nothing but defiance and sarcasm in her demeanor. Lisa was someone that Sergio cared about, someone that should have protected him; but she didn't. Bobby had been abusing Lisa, and when the physical abuse escalated to the point that my son became aware of the situation, he stepped forward and confronted the abuser. The killer, a known gang member, gathered two carloads of his "people" and ambushed my son. Bobby was seen at times bragging about his gang affiliation by showing gang initials tattooed across his stomach and when he would throw up gang signs at altercations. My son stood up for what he believed in and it cost him his life. Instead of taking this opportunity to break free from her tormentor, Lisa defended the killer, aided and abetted him, and even testified on his behalf during the trial. Her betrayal has been difficult to live with. We were dealing with a group of life-long criminals with lengthy criminal records that know how to work the justice system and whose vicious acts have escalated to killing a person. A two-strike felon and the group of villains that helped him will always be responsible for Sergio's death.

A lot of our family members offered their moral support by being present at both the preliminary and actual trial; although all of the family members that were on our side of the case held regular jobs and so their attendance was inconsistent. In contrast, the opposing side had members in their group that did not hold steady jobs and therefore attended regularly. I know it was a great sacrifice for most of our friends and family to have taken time off work to be there for us and to endure such a difficult situation; I am immensely grateful for their support.

I made some blue ribbons that we wanted to wear in the court- room to show our support for Sergio. However, we were asked to remove them because it could potentially sway the jury, or it could be perceived that it swayed the jury and it may be grounds for appeals in the event of a conviction. On the other hand, the killer was consis- tently allowed to walk into the courtroom with a bible in his hand… would that not sway the jury? The blatant disregard for the victim or the victim's rights and unbalanced due process, was appalling and at times very difficult to endure.

Months of harassment and intimidation tactics became the norm for these people in efforts to keep anyone from testifying. "I'm glad he's dead, I'm glad he died," the assailants taunted us daily as we relived Sergio's death through the trial. At one point, before the trial, I received a letter that the killer had sent to my brother; in this letter he wrote things that disturbed me for some time. In that letter, which he named, "The night three people died," he talked about 'respect' as if he actually believed in it or remotely deserved it. He wrote, "If the deceased mother could of put all her energy into having patience with her son and keep giving chances to him no matter what…Her energy is out there full blast, doing what is necessary to give her some type of calmness in her sorrow" [sic[1]]. He was referring to my efforts of trying to track him down while he was a fugitive.

This criminal dared to judge me for the times I argued with my son and held him accountable for his behavior, and for giving Sergio the freedom to choose his own actions. He offered parental advice although he is not a parent. He is oblivious as to what it takes to be a good parent, no idea of the sacrifices and harsh decisions that a parent is faced with through the years. I had only two brief conversations with him the entire time I knew him, certainly not long enough to get to know a person; who is he to cast judgment on me?

Of course, Bobby would not understand this because he has no respect for anyone or anything, including the law. In this letter he admitted that he has "a rap sheet longer than myself, plus three years of high-risk parole." He added that he "worked so hard to beat the system." He seemed to be doing that very well in this trial. He lied, manipulated, and played on the emotions of the jury. In the letter, the killer even stated that Sergio was brave and that he had a lot of potential. The killer went so far as to quote a Bible verse: *"An eye for an eye, and a tooth for a tooth"* (Matthew 5:38). It seemed obvious to me that he was taking revenge for my son confronting him a week or so prior to the homicide.

I wonder now—what would the killer think if I were to take the same approach? What if I were to kill the killer? Would my fate be the

same as his? Would society condemn me or would they condone my actions? Faced with the opportunity to avenge my son's death, would I do it? Would I take another man's life in an effort to kill the pain I feel inside? I sigh because I know that nothing will ever change what happened, that no one will ever be able to take the pain away, even if the killer were dead; even if all of them were dead. That's the difference between a decent person and a killer—he failed to recognize that once Sergio was gone, that his own life would not get better, even if he were to get acquitted because no matter what happens, he will always live with the fact that he killed a man. He would still be the same miserable person, would continue to abuse my sister, plus have legal consequences on top of everything else; or is he above the law? Is he so experienced at this that he could fool a jury to the point of a full acquittal?

My niece Monique, the one we took into our home when she was a few years younger, spewed vile lies about Sergio during her testimony and she went as far as to say that she loved Sergio and would never lie. She used the fact that we took her into our home as proof, so, "Why would I lie?" she asked during cross examination. I can't begin to tell you how appalling this was to me as I sat there and listened as she gave such distorted testimony.

My sister and the killer both testified under oath that they had been married just a few weeks before the altercation; this was a complete fabrication. They went to the extent of falsifying a legal document. They produced a phony Mexican marriage certificate they submitted to the court upon the Assistant District Attorney's request for proof. A representative from that Mexican State later concluded that the document was a fake. However, the (ADA) failed to line up a witness from the Registro Civil (Civil Records) office in Mexico that supposedly recorded the marriage. I was livid on the first day of the trial when the ADA dropped that bomb on me, saying that he was not able to get anyone to testify regarding the legitimacy of that marriage because he had not looked into it until just before the trial. I had specifically reminded him a month before, to which he responded that he had it all under control. But now we were stuck. He would not even ask for a continuance in order to secure the witness because he said he did not want to leave an open door for an appeal. The defense delayed the trial for months with repeated continuances, yet we could not ask for one, one that could prove that the defendant and his co-conspirators had lied under oath. All he did was ask me to call that office in Mexico and find out for sure if the document was false. Of course, I did that right away, and the clerk at the civil registration office confirmed that that marriage was not valid. She said that the page and book number listed on that certificate did not even exist.

The ADA did argue the matter profusely as he knew that would be a crucial element in the case. I rationalized that if they would go to such great lengths to falsify a marriage certificate, why not a toxicology report as well? That too was something the ADA did not debate but I had complete confidence in him. The homicide detective told us that this particular ADA had the best reputation for prosecuting gang-related homicides. It was obvious that the news about this phony marriage caught everyone by surprise when my sister blurted it out. The look on the defense attorney was epic! He began to stutter as he struggled to buy time to come up with something to say on something that he was not prepared to handle at that moment. This was during Lisa's testimony at the preliminary trial. I can't even remember what brought on that subject but the ADA requested a copy of that marriage certificate, which was later produced at the actual trial. The judge quickly

informed her that she had the right not to testify against her "hus-band" so as not to incriminate him. I was just as amazed as everyone in the courtroom, but I knew for a fact that it was all a lie. I was more amazed though, at the eagerness in which she stated that she wanted to waive her rights because she wanted to testify on Bobby's behalf. I think the reason she came up with that is to use all that conjugal vis-itation time to devise their strategy for an acquittal. I don't think she expected that she would be asked to produce the original certificate as the look on her face gave the impression that she was taken aback by the request.

With all the other strange things that happened, I truly believe it's not beyond the realm of possibility that crimes were committed to cover up or plant evidence. How else was my son's clothing lost? They suddenly came up with a knife they claimed belonged to Sergio but it was not submitted into evidence on the night of the homicide nor at the preliminary trial. Their explanation was that they did not trust the police with it. Bobby, the killer, testified that "I didn't see it but, in my mind, I pictured a knife." During his testimony, it was confirmed that Sergio was unarmed during the stabbing. Why then was it allowed into evidence at the actual trial when it was not mentioned previously? Why did the ADA not push to run fingerprints on it? None of these details were allowed into court and this would potentially sway the jury's opinion, allowing them to see the killer in a much more favor-able light. I was really surprised that Bobby had taken the stand to tes-tify. I am reminded of the unyielding pressure from the ADA as I recently read the court transcripts regarding Bobby's testimony of the following in an exchange during cross-examination:

"ADA: Well, you understand that you're the one that implanted that knife in Sergio's chest, don't you?

Bobby: Yes.

ADA: So, in other words, Sergio was stabbed by you?

Bobby: Yes.

ADA: And you told the witness?

Bobby: I still can't believe it, but it was me."

Bobby tried to rephrase his statements and he later claimed he saw black spots at the moment that he stabbed Sergio. He claimed that he was very afraid of Sergio even prior to the altercation yet he failed to explain why he did not call the police or 911 for help. At one point during the ADA's cross-examination, Bobby tried to blame his own brother for killing Sergio but that allegation was quickly abolished by the ADA's arguments.

We all felt optimistic about a conviction; particularly after Bobby took the stand; we felt we had a strong case. The ADA explained that because the killer was a 2-strike felon, that having the indictment be for first-degree murder would give us leeway as the jury would be able to have options for lower charges such as second-degree, voluntary manslaughter, but he said that even an involuntary manslaughter conviction would secure a life sentence. The ADA felt optimistic, particularly because the defense offered a plea bargain several times. They offered a 15-year plea, and although optimistic, the ADA strongly suggested we consider accepting it. I understood the plea offer to mean that the defense was feeling insecure with the way the trial was going and I stood firm on refusing any plea bargain. My husband on the other hand, suggested we take it… but I refused. I was not willing to bargain on what I felt strongly about… the killer deserved life in

prison. I had faith and I was optimistic.

The killer's sister Chela had also been part of the altercation the night my son was killed. A vile woman with a life filled with violence and turmoil. She was part of the group that arrived at my mother's house and had participated in the altercation by instigating and pushing my mother to the ground. This is a woman who had not yet reached middle age, pushing an older woman as part of the plot. Chela had testified that she was so drunk that night that she vomited all over herself. Her son Baltazar, my niece Monique's lover, was also part of the group. As they rushed into their ambush against Sergio that night, Baltazar got out of the car with a bat in his hand. During the testimony, it was revealed that my brother Raymond had called Baltazar on the phone after the criminals fled the crime scene. Raymond had been told that threatening phone calls to the witnesses were being made by the assailants. After reaching Baltazar on the phone, and after several attemts to get Baltazar to understand that family was being hurt, Raymond told him, "My nephew Sergio has just been killed. You guys have done enough damage; stop with the threatening phone calls."

Baltazar replied, "Fuck your nephew!"

After hearing this testimony, my husband looked to me and with tears in his eyes said, "Sergio never had a chance against all those evil people." I can't image what must have gone through Sergio's head; seeing all these people there with the purpose of hurting others and seeing his grandmother thrown to the ground, I am sure it all played a big part in the brawl.

Some of the memories of the trial proceedings are still very vivid, while others I have chosen to suppress because they are simply too painful. I vaguely recall the judge, although obviously experienced at his job he seemed affected by some of the testimony. At one point, after the defense attorney was carrying on and on trying to vilify my son to no end. The judge looked over at me as he heard me cry. The judge then slammed his gavel loudly as he turned to the defense attorney and, I am paraphrasing as I recall he said "Enough, I have heard enough. Will you not consider the grief of this mother? Must you subject her to more of this nonsense?"

My husband and I attended every court hearing, with or without our family and friends. I did not dare look directly at the jury as we were instructed not to. I wanted to look at their reactions to certain testimony but I had to force myself to contain my impulses. Although they could clearly see us because we were seated in the section next to them, it was difficult to gauge how they were processing the evidence presented. To this day, I can remember a couple of the jury members; one in particular was a middle aged man that usually sat in the back row. I noticed he would look in our direction at times and I felt the weight of his stare; but more than that, I felt compassion emanating from his intent stare.

Detective Levinns was one of the lead homicide detectives assigned to the case, he was kind and considerate, quite different from his partner, Detective Brackpool. Detective Levinns attended most of the court appearances during the indictment, preliminary, and at the actual trial. He would meet us in the parking lot and would walk us to the courthouse because he understood our concern for our safety.

He made every effort to keep us informed of the process and aware of potential risks in the case. My husband and I did not miss any part of the testimony except when the autopsy was going to be presented, Detective Levinns approached me and kindly said, "I know you want to be here but I strongly suggest you step outside for this

part of the trial." I was reluctant at first and he looked at me and came closer as he said softly, he whispered almost, "This will be very, very painful for you, and I want to protect you from that." With glossy eyes he continued and his voice broke when he said, "Please let me protect you from that." I felt in my heart that there was nothing anyone could ever show me about my son that would ever make me quiver. I longed for his bloody shirt when he was taken to the ER, and I even felt envy for the doctors that got to hold his heart in their hands; nothing could ever make me see him in a different light. Nevertheless, I understood what the detective was trying to tell me and I figured that after all his years of experience in this, he must know what he's talking about, so I agreed to wait outside with my husband. Everyone was in there, everyone but my husband and me. That day we did not have family or friends with us, it was just the two of us, and I felt that I had left my son in there alone with only the ADA and the Detective to represent Sergio, to speak on his behalf and to be present for him in front of the jury.

It seemed like an eternity before that session was over and when the detective finally came out, he approached and cleared his throat before he spoke. He didn't say much, just that it was "said and done." It was all in the hands of the jury…and then, all we could do was wait.

Closing Thought
"Never leave anything to chance or trust in others to cover every angle; nobody will ever care about a conviction more than you, because this is your loss."

---

[1] sic—means content left as in original source.

Chapter Seven

THE VERDICT

Assembled once again in the courtroom after several days of jury deliberations, we were notified that the jury had reached a verdict. I was appalled when I saw the guilty praying for mercy, after showing us none. I recalled in my mind the verses found in (Psalms 5:9-10) *Not a word from their mouth can be trusted; their heart is filled with malice. Their throat is an open grave; with their tongues they tell lies. Declare them guilty, O God."*

I was determined to hold on to my faith; I kept telling myself that God would give us justice, that He would see their evil hearts and would not let them hurt anyone else.

We arrived at the courthouse within a half hour from hearing that the jury had reached a verdict. I wanted to pray for the jury and the courtroom before anyone went in there so I made my way into the room, with no one around, or so I thought, I went to the side of the room by the area where the jury would sit; I touched the railing and walked slowly, praying as I walked. I prayed that God would give them wisdom and that they would not make a decision based on emotions. I can still remember that musty smell of the courtroom, the heavy wood moldings and benches that seemed to scream at me the history of the countless criminal trials it had housed since its inception. I cried as I prayed, and I called on Jesus for strength and courage to survive what would happen next. As I turned to leave the room, I noticed that one of the bodyguards was sitting silently by the door. He had followed me in without me noticing him; he heard my prayers, he saw me cry, he felt my pain as was evident by the tears I noticed streaming down his face.

As the jury prepared to announce the verdict, all the anxiety and stress began to take its toll on me. I began to shake and cry in anticipation of the verdict. This, too, was one more layer that I had to endure, but it was "almost over," I kept telling myself.

Just moments before the jury made their announcement; I changed my mind about taking the plea bargain the defense had previously offered. I gestured to the ADA to come over and as he approached, I hesitantly told him, between gasps "Tell them that we'll take it." He asked, "How much time?" and I answered, "Twenty." At which point, he went over to the defense, looked the accused in the eyes and relayed the information. I saw the accused shake his head in disagreement...and refusal as he looked straight at me. At the last minute, I had changed my mind to accept a plea...and at the last minute, he changed his mind not to.

I felt my heart pounding so loudly that I was certain everyone in the courtroom could hear it. My breathing became forced as my whole body became tense. At one point I felt like I was going to be sick as I realized the significance of the moment and I came to terms with the fact that there would be no turning back...that no matter the outcome, I would have to live with the decision of that verdict for the rest of my life. I thought to myself, "God be with us...here we go, please hold my hand!"

I held hands and prayed with my husband and my friend Traci just before the verdict was read. The jury foreman read the verdict on all charges—one by one—"On the count of Murder in the First Degree, we, the jury, find the defendant... Not Guilty!" And worse, they found him not guilty on all the charges. It was then that my faith was shaken. I felt on that day that God granted them mercy and denied us justice, the justice that I desperately needed. It added to our tragedy and loss. I remember screaming, "No, oh God, no!" And immediately I heard loud cheers coming from the killer's family. I looked in the direction of the killer and I saw him raise both his hands in the air as he yelled "Yeah!," as if to celebrate another win in his book. I then heard my sister and my niece cheer, but I dared not look in their direction because I was at the end of my rope and I felt sure I would probably faint. I was shaking like the night we were told my son had died, and like the next day when I saw him at the morgue; I was deeply confused and felt an overwhelming sense of betrayal; betrayal from my sister and betrayal from my niece. But what was most agonizing was feeling that God, too, had betrayed us; God had turned away from us.

I felt abandoned by Him, yet I thought of (Romans 8:28) *"And we know that all things work together for good to them that love God, to them who are the called according to His purpose."* I wondered what good could come out from the loss of my son and the acquittal, and what is God's purpose in all of this? Seeking justice for Sergio had kept me moving forward. This verdict didn't make sense to me. How would I go on without my son, without justice, and how could I possibly stop the unrelenting sorrow and bleeding of my own heart?

The accused was acquitted; he got away with killing my son while we were left to serve a life sentence of pain and sorrow. A criminal is free today because he knew how to manipulate the system. As we exited the courtroom, I softly said to myself, "No matter how much they change their lives or how sincerely they repent…if ever; all their lives put together could never make up for Sergio's alone."

I had prepared a victim's impact statement a few days before the

verdict was read as the ADA said I would be allowed to address the court and the killer in the event of a conviction. He stated this was an opportunity to express how the homicide has affected us and to shed some light into the magnitude of our loss. He said that at times these statements are taken into account when determining sentencing. I pulled this statement out of my box of archives. I did not get the opportunity to say it then but I can say it now:

Victim Impact Statement:

My name is Sandra and I stand before this court today on behalf of my family to represent our beloved Sergio and seeking justice for his wrongful death. I will try to summarize the impact that his death brought upon our life when he was tragically killed by this man, the accused "Bobby," (full name omitted).

One of Sergio's friends once told me that it was easy to like Sergio and to be his friend and that you'd have to try really hard not to like him because he was a really good guy and great friend.

Sergio was savagely killed at the hands of this criminal. In our hearts, Sergio died a hero because he died as a result of defending his aunt.

Let me assure you that for a parent, there is no such thing as closure. Losing a child through illness or by accident is painful enough, but losing a child at the hands of a killer is absolutely devastating. How can a parent go on living when your child has been viciously attacked and killed... gone forever. For us the pain is much too real, it is every moment of every day and it will remain that way forever.

His death has brought tears upon tears, profound pain, sleepless nights, severed family ties, and a world full of sadness. We are now forced to find a way to survive through many layers of grief caused by his shocking death. Not a day goes by that I don't cry for my son, and not a day goes by that I don't wish this had never happened.

It's offensive to see the mockery that the defense attorney has made out of this trial and the ridiculous arguments and justifications presented for what this man has done; although a confessed killer, to try to justify his actions and minimize the loss of a human life is absolutely intolerable. I have sat here and listened to the

absurd testimony of the same people that Sergio defended, stood up for, and trusted. To sit here and listen to their attempt to taint my son's name even after all damage and pain they have already caused; it is simply repulsive. Sergio was not perfect, but neither is anyone in this courtroom and he did not deserve to die such a horrific and violent death.

I owe it to Sergio to tell you that this is also about watching Sergio grow up to be a loving and giving young man and feeling proud when I stood next to him.

It's about realizing that he's gone forever and not wanting to accept his death; knowing that this act of violence has terribly changed our lives; feeling anger and frustration for not being able to change what was done to Sergio.

It's about mustering all the courage you have to tell my first-born son that his brother had just been killed and feeling like a villain for breaking his heart.

It's being told that the killer had fled and feeling appalled at his cowardice.

It's about being absolutely horrified by seeing my child's body lying on a cold table, his life taken from him... his warmth gone forever. It's telling him the final and most painful "I love you," through a glass wall as I was forbidden to come near him.

It's about crying beyond consolation when I sat in his room trying to select the clothing he was to wear for his funeral.

It's about watching grown men weep and fall apart before my eyes because the grief is too much that even they can't bear it.

It's feeling the rage when I get his autopsy report and reading the gruesome details of the injuries inflicted and cause of death...feeling sick to my stomach for the evil done against him; not done by mistake.

It's about continuous and offensive harassment from his family members that respected no boundaries or

gave no sympathy or compassion for our family, even during the initial mourning period.

It's about the first Thanksgiving without him, visiting his grave because I did not want him to be alone. Then sitting around the dinner table that night with somber faces and heavy hearts; crying as we say grace and choking on the thought of the words spoken by Sergio the year before when he said, "I am thankful that I'm here with my family."

It's about wanting to skip Christmas altogether because it will be too painful. Forcing myself for my other kids; hanging every ornament on that tree with tears, wishing he were still here with us.

It's about going to the first court appearance and seeing the killer's face and feeling rage as I saw his arrogance and insolence, but not remorse.

It's about taking a stand for what is right. Sergio's love and courage made him who he was. I stand for Sergio now, because I know that he would do the same for me.

It's ironic that Bobby killed Sergio by stabbing him in the heart, and it was Sergio's big heart that defined his character. I believe that it was precisely that which threatened Bobby the most for he knew that Sergio cared enough to defend those around him from people like Bobby.

It's also about my opportunity to address the killer face to face and say, "I know you have no regrets or conviction for what you have done. You are only sorry that you got caught and inconvenienced by all this. We all know that you would have never confronted Sergio alone because you are a coward and that is why you called for help. You had the power to diffuse the situation, you being that much older than him; but you chose to kill him instead because that is who you are, a killer. I pray that one day you come to acquire a conscience, only then will you realize the enormity of what you have done. When 'an eye for an eye' means giving up your soul, you are at the very bottom of humanity and that

which is the lowest form of life.
Neither your life nor the lives of all
those involved in the homicide would
ever make up for Sergio's life but I
hope that his death weighs on you for
the remainder of your pathetic existence."

Your Honor, I would now like to
address you and respectfully say that
instead of vengeance we ask that you,
the Judge would sentence Bobby to
life without the possibility of parole
and remember the rights of the victim
as you consider the proper measure of
justice. I quote from the Bible verse
found in Proverbs 24:23-35: *"These also
are sayings of the wise: to show partiality in
judging is not good. Whoever says to the
guilty 'you are innocent'-people will curse him
and nations denounce him. But it will go well
with those who convict the guilty, and rich
blessings will come upon them."*

I would love to have the jury that found him Not Guilty hear
about this verse and read this book now. I wonder if after knowing
all the background that was not allowed into court would change
their perspective; I seriously doubt they would have the conscience
to declare the same verdict.

The jury failed to make the right decision and I learned the inner workings of the justice system. So careful to protect the rights of the accused, it forgot about my son. Sergio had no voice, no second chance. I am his voice now, I will not be silent…let me be heard. Let me give testimony to his character and his life.

Closing Thought
"I began to shake and cry in anticipation of the verdict.
This was yet another layer I had to endure. "

Chapter Eight

THE OBSESSION

I became obsessed with reliving every detail of the trial. I had to know what went wrong. I pondered every possible action. I dwelled on them day and night; I was consumed with anger and sorrow; tormented by the inability to do anything about that situation. I felt guilty for not taking the plea bargain initially offered.

I couldn't live with myself; I felt I had let Sergio down. I hated myself and those that took his life. I kept thinking, "I need to do something, I had to fix it somehow"…I simply couldn't live with the overwhelming weight of it all.

Every decision would carry life-changing consequences, and out of respect for my children, I will not mention those deep dark thoughts. Suffice it to say, however, that at those moments I understood exactly what Job (Job 3: 1-3, 20-26) meant when he talked about cursing the day he was born. For you see, having never been born is significantly different than wishing to die. Now I have a family that depends on me, and dying would cause them pain, more pain. Day and night I prayed that God would make that crippling pain stop and that it would all just be a nightmare.

I wondered if this was some horrible punishment for something in my past…but no, it wouldn't be fair that my child would pay for anything I might have done. What then? Was my faith not sufficient? Was it not deep or pure enough? I lived in that torment for many months and I prayed, "Oh God, forgive me if my spirit faltered at any moment during this trial."

I hated myself and began to doubt every decision I had ever made and everything I told the attorney during the trial. I wondered if I had done enough or said enough. I wondered why the assistant district attorney did not call me to testify. And why he dropped the ball on several crucial elements of the case? Why were certain facts not admitted into court; such as hearing that the killer had been involved in a similar stabbing prior to my son's death, or the possibility that perhaps the autopsy report could have been manipulated? I still wonder how they were able to get a copy of the report long before we did and if they had inside sources that facilitated such matters.

Conversely, why were certain things allowed into court that that should not have been? Why was it all right for the court to seemingly disregard the victim's rights and my son's life in favor of protecting the rights of a killer? It was exhausting trying to figure out if it was I that failed to provide the prosecutor enough information or if he had failed to do his best, but ultimately it all came down to the jury's decision, and I believe it was the jury members that failed to give us justice for a killing that was admitted and unjustified.

My entire perspective in life changed, and I became afraid to plan for the future because I was painfully aware of how fragile life is and that everything can change in an instant. I was jaded by the lack of trust that now reined in my mind. I could no longer do the normal things I did and enjoyed prior to Sergio's death; I lost my capability to do even the simplest of things, such as put on makeup and cook a meal. I felt so lost and out of place no matter where I was. Up until this trial I had considered myself a fairly intelligent woman but now, I question my own consciousness.

For a long time I was left doubting my role in my son's life, asking myself if I had made a positive impact on his existence. Was I everything I could have been for him? Did I provide him with all the right tools to be successful in life? Was I there for him every time he needed me? I was tormented by the "what if's." What if I would've picked him up right after we last spoke on the phone instead of waiting to meet him the next day? What if I had been there when the altercation ensued? I would have gladly taken the blow for him. What if I had been able to make it by his side when he was gasping for air? What if I could have saved him using CPR or putting pressure on the wound? What if I had prevented him from removing the knife from his chest – would that have made a difference? What if I had testified? What if I had taken the plea bargain? What if, what if, what if—I was driving myself insane with the incessant what ifs.

In all honesty, I still struggle with this sometimes but now I have realized that we all have to die, that life on earth is not eternal and one by one, we all must die. It helps to think that our loved ones are fine in their new realm; it is us, the survivors that are left behind that suffer the most. We experience the loss and are forced to find a "new normal."

Years after this tragedy, as I gathered all the notes I had written through the years, and prepared to write this book, I found the old journal in which I had written some of the first episodes of the aftermath that we experienced through this heartache.

Reading through this journal I ran across a few notes that I entered during the first year after Sergio died, and reading through those pages opened up the pit of despair again as I recounted the feelings that I had tried to expel from me and unto those pages when I wrote them, word for word I see evidence of the tears that had fallen on those pages, and I notice the dates scribbled at the top of each entry and I realize how much time has gone by. But you wouldn't know it by the sorrow that still remains. I read page by page and recounted those memories so vividly described in the journal that it forced me right back to those moments in time where the wound was so raw, so deep and my soul so distraught.

I flip back to the pages at the beginning of this nightmare and ponder on my supplication for justice before and during the trial. I see the prayers I wrote in my journal during each day of the court proceedings. I wrote about the harassment, intimidation, and threats made to us and our extended family by those people. I came to a section in the journal that reads "I admit that I am afraid when I walk into the courtroom because of those people and I wonder how much worse things will get before this is all over."

So I hang on to the verse in the Bible found in (Deut. 32:43) *"Rejoice, you nations, with his people, for he will avenge the blood of his servants; he will take vengeance on his enemies and make atonement for his land and people,"* I find strength and hope in that verse. Many years later I am saddened to see how much hope I had for justice, but justice did not prevail for us, at least not in the way we hoped, not in this world... not yet.

Immediately after the devastating news that my son had died, I went through the normal stages of shock, grief, anger, sadness, and solitude. However, it doesn't end at the funeral. When all the friends, family, and visitors had gone, we were left alone and forced to face an unimaginable grief. I felt utterly alone as I dealt with the demons that tormented me day and night; constant shadows that followed me wherever I went, relentlessly pursuing me and dominating my every thought. I was exhausted to the point where I was oblivious to everything around me, including my other kids. Thoughts of my son, his life, and his death were constantly on my mind; many times I wondered how I would be able to survive. Thoughts about the killer, his brutal actions, and his evil heart crept, unwelcomed, into my mind; thoughts of my sister Lisa and my niece Monique, and their unwavering support for the killer, abandoning the rest of us in the process. I was letting those demons take over areas of my life that were most important to me.

But I too was at fault of perpetuating this anguish, by unintentionally feeding those demons with my doubts, guilt, and anger, so much so, that it became such a daunting task to lead a normal life; the thought of healing seemed unimaginable, the prospect of happiness felt unattainable.

Along the way I realized that even when I was trying to walk it alone and away from God...He never left me! Just because God is invisible doesn't mean He isn't there. He walked beside me and carried me in my weakest moments, even when I didn't think I wanted Him to. He was there because He loves me. Although I felt insignificant in the grander scheme of things and I felt God was too busy for me and my pain, I was reminded by the scriptures that Pastor Raul would preach on; in this case the Trinity came to mind. As is written *"In the beginning was the Word, and the Word was with God, and the Word was God."* John 1:1. This tells me that He is an army in and of Himself. We don't need anything or anyone else; that nothing is too great or too difficult for Him.

He is Omnipresent *"7 Whither shall I go from thy spirit? or whither shall I flee from thy presence? 8 If I ascend up into heaven, thou art there: if I make my bed in hell, behold, thou art there. 9 If I take the wings of the morning, and dwell in the uttermost parts of the sea; 10 Even there shall thy hand lead*

me, and thy right hand shall hold me," (Psalms 139:7-10). He is Omnipotent *"Alleluia: for the Lord God omnipotent reigneth,"* (Rev. 19:6.) And He is Omniscient *"12 For the word of God is quick, and powerful, and sharper than any two edged sword, piercing even to the dividing asunder of soul and spirit, and of the joints and marrow, and is a discerner of the thoughts and intents of the heart,"* (Heb. 4:12).

All these passages helped me realize that God is in complete control. That I cannot run or hide from Him, that He knows my past, present, future, and He knows even how I would react to this tragedy and what I would do with it.

Despite it all, He chose me to be the mother of this young man that would one day experience a violent death. He understood what I would go through, even when I ran from Him, and in His infinite wisdom He trusted me to do the right thing and come back to Him. He trusted my strength more than I did myself. He believed in me with greater insight than my limited mind could comprehend. Just because I couldn't feel Him near me, doesn't mean He couldn't feel me or my pain.

Was the acquittal a test to see what we would do with that verdict? Surely God knew how I would react, but perhaps He wanted to give me the opportunity to experience it anyway, because this would carve deeper into my wound and into my spirit—right down to my core. Would I then choose to either abandon my faith in God and become a bitter and repulsive carcass, an unsightly human being dragging myself in the misery of my despair.

Or would I chose to renew my faith and commitment to God with greater reverence, and total dependency on Him; or in God's infinite wisdom, knowing that my faith would falter and that I would attempt to walk through that suffering alone, He would allow me to experience first-hand what it would be like.

I remember during the first few days after my son was killed, feeling the agony of such grief—knowing that would have to be the ultimate depth of sorrow I would ask myself how those people that do not know the Lord could ever survive through such pain. Could it be then that God heard those thoughts and knew what His purpose for me would be? If so, He may have felt I needed to also experience the pain of the acquittal so He could equip me completely when my time came to begin this ministry. Only then could I have greater insight into that travesty as well so that I would fully come to know the hopelessness and deprivation that comes from not having God in our heart—and that would have to be the biggest tragedy of all. Either way, it brought me to a greater understanding, appreciation, and compassion for those people walking through this journey of grief without God's love and strength.

However, I knew that before I could begin to help others I had to help myself by finding productive ways that would help me heal inside; that would help mend my heart and quiet my soul. I needed to once again feel that I was a good mother and wife.

It was important for me to be able to look at myself in the mirror and be okay with who I saw in that reflection. I realized that it's not about how broken I am, but rather what I chose to do with the pieces, that matters..

During those dreadful months after the trial, I could not even look at myself without feeling I had failed Sergio. I am reminded of the Bible verse which says, *"Now we see but a poor reflection as in a mirror; then we shall see face to face. Now I know in part; then I shall know fully, even as I am fully known."* (1 Cor. 13:12). I am painfully aware that we don't have all the answers here on Earth and that it will all be revealed when

In order for me to break free from the shackles that bound me in torment, I had to seek God. All healing takes time, and healing from this type of pain is no different, in fact, it is worse. It took time and continuous effort.

we are in the presence of the Lord. *"So we fix our eyes not on what is seen, but on what is unseen. For what is seen is temporary, but what is unseen is eternal,"* (2 Cor. 4:18.) And finally, *"we live by faith, not by sight."* (2 Cor. 5:7).

In order for me to break free from the shackles that bound me in that tormented state, I had to seek God. All healing takes time, and healing from this type of pain is no different, in fact it is worse. It took time and continuous effort. I felt that I had to step outside myself in order to think clearly; I began to go to support group meetings, and although some left me feeling worse than when I went in, others were more positive in the way they conducted the meetings and that helped give me some level of comfort and hope. My husband and I attended a few groups before we found a couple that we were able to connect with, Parents of Murdered Children and The Compassionate Friends. We soon met people that had walked our same path. We finally felt that we were not alone in this painful journey, as others had obviously learned to survive such a devastating loss and some had also survived a murder trial. For the most part, though, we found that people are just people and we all are simply human—with flaws and weaknesses—and that we don't have all the answers and that we all have different tolerance levels but together we can help make a difference in each other's lives. First, though, we had to be willing to surrender our grief in exchange for peace and hope. And by that time, we were more than willing to do it.

Aside from the physical, emotional, and mental trauma we lived through, we also experienced a financial strain, as would be expected. After months of healing and deep soul searching, I considered other possible reasons for the acquittal: a) That God would grant them mercy to see what they would do with it and test their faith against the prayers they fervently prayed just moments before the verdict was

announced; b) Because of the nature of this case and the real threat against our family, I wonder if it's beyond the realm of possibility that God allowed the killer to be acquitted in order to prevent further harm to us. I say that because of the harassment that transpired before and during the trial. We had to walk into the courthouse with two bodyguards, and we did not allow our other children to attend the hearings and trial. The risk was real, and the trauma was unbearable.

I prayed for God's peace in helping me not think about my son's death as much, for Him to fill my heart with peace and quiet my soul so that I could survive. Slowly I began to get involved in grief support activities, and it helped to know that I was helping others so my desire to continue on that path grew. I now look at it as an opportunity to give back. When I die I want my legacy to be that I helped shape the character of my children in a positive way, that I was a good role model in their life, and that the sacrifices we made as parents were all for their well-being. I want to stand before my Maker and hear Him say, *"Well done, good and faithful servant,"* (Matthew 25:21). I want to know that when I leave this earth, I exhausted all that's within me to help make a difference in someone's life. That I learned from the loss of my son not to take life for granted and to cherish every moment with our loved ones; that I got a second chance to be a better parent, more in-tuned with the needs of my children instead of placing such high standards for them that perhaps are unrealistic, and to balance my priorities. I learned to listen more and to choose which battles were worth fighting, to let my kids be kids. To focus on those items that dealt with honor, love, and morals and let go of some of the more trivial matters such as, the color my daughter would choose to dye her hair. Guess what? Hair actually grows back! I discovered that I had to let them be who they needed to be and respect their individuality to a much greater degree.

I further realized that I had to grow in certain areas of my life that would help make me a more wholesome person. I was also determined not to compromise on my Godly beliefs and to stand true and firm to my values. I recognize the pressures from society that can derail my best intentions and steer me in the wrong direction. I had to start saying no to projects that were not within the parameters of my goals or that would hinder my walk with the Lord. I began to think about how I could simplify my life so I could enjoy it in a more meaningful way. Some of the Bible verses that give me peace about the whole trial and killer now are: (Psalms 7:9-17 NIV)

9O righteous God, who searches minds and hearts, bring to an end the violence of the wicked and make the righteous secure.

10My shield is God Most High, who saves the upright in heart.

11God is a righteous judge, a God who expresses his wrath every day.

12If he does not relent, he will sharpen his sword; he will bend and string his bow.

13He has prepared his deadly weapons; he makes ready his flaming arrows.

14He who is pregnant with evil and conceives trouble gives birth to disillusionment.

15He who digs a hole and scoops it out falls

into the pit he has made.

*16The trouble he causes recoils on himself;
his violence comes down on his own head.*

*17I will give thanks to the LORD because of
his righteousness and will sing praise to the
name of the LORD Most High."*

Another verse that helps give me hope that the wicked will one day be held accountable is Romans 12:19 (KJV) *"Dearly beloved, avenge not yourselves, but rather give place unto wrath: for it is written, Vengeance is mine; I will repay, saith the Lord."*

I take comfort in knowing that God is the Master Judge and that the killer will one day stand before Him and give an account of his actions. On that day, he will be alone, without his conspirators, and he will not be able to deceive the Lord Most High. On that day, justice will be served. But until that day we hold firm to the truths of the Lord and the promises of eternity and the hope that we will be reunited with our beloved.

Not one day goes by that I don't think of Sergio; in fact, there are many days when I miss him so much that the pain creeps up all over again and I find myself sobbing, there in the middle of whatever I am doing or wherever I am. In our "new normal," we must go on, live life and experience moments without him. He missed his older brother's wedding, where he was to be the best man. He missed the birth of his first niece and nephew. He missed his sister's wedding, and he missed being present at the celebration of his baby brother for achieving his Eagle Scout rank.

Even eight years later, at times, the pain can still feel like it was just yesterday. However, it is no longer the majority of the time; time itself has helped the healing process. Healing takes place in different forms. There are times when I wonder what if healing comes from forcing ourselves to carry on, and then perhaps joy may follow with effort and determination. I have found that staying busy really helps, and that helping others helps me heal inside. There are many parents with sad stories about their deceased children. Each story is painful to hear. My son was a caring and selfless young man who loved to help others; somehow I feel a connection to him through the charity work that I do, and it helps keep me going because I want him to be proud of me and of the person I've become.

His death is the worst thing that I have ever had to suffer through, but I am determined to use that horrific tragedy to powerfully impact our lives and the lives of others. I speak of suffering because in addition to the emotional grief, I have also lived with chronic pain for over fifteen years now. I had three brain surgeries within a 5-year period for a condition that prevents me from doing many activities that I used to enjoy. The recovery period after each of these surgeries was agonizing and no matter how hard I tried to expedite the healing process, I had to learn to be patient and endure until I was better. I had to learn to modify my life in ways that would still allow me to be productive and self-sufficient, but I still struggle with pain daily. I wake up with a headache and I go to bed with a headache, and while some days are much worse than others, living with chronic pain has made me value life and not take things for granted.

My husband also suffers from chronic pain and he, too, has learned to live with our altered physical state as well as with an altered emotional state caused by the loss of our son. My husband has had to overcome many difficulties to maintain a productive lifestyle and to provide for his family. A series of trial-and-error experiences have led to lifestyle adjustments that work best for us. We had to find new methods within his physical limitations, which we still finds challenging.

I was inspired by a conversation that my husband had with an old friend during the days following the funeral. His friend gave his heartfelt condolences, and then said to my husband, "I would hate to be in your shoes, I can't imagine what you are going through." My husband replied, "These are the shoes that God has me walking in now, and I have to walk in them. I do not want to take any medication to numb the pain as I feel I have to feel every bit of it because it's just how much I love my son. I was filled with happiness at his birth and wanted to feel every minute of that joy. I also need to feel every minute of the pain caused by his death."

Indeed, we never did take any of the medication or anti-depressants that the doctors offered, our medicine came from God—the master healer—creator of our body, mind, and spirit. We believed that taking medication would simply numb the pain, and therefore delay the healing process. We felt the full impact of our pain right from the start, but I certainly don't recommend that everyone take this approach. There are certainly situations where the medications are needed, after all, God allowed them to be discovered and developed. I can only share with you our reasons and perspectives, but each person should make their own decision and seek the help of a licensed medical professional if necessary.

We were well grounded in the Lord and I can guarantee you—had that not been the case—I would not have taken the same approach. I don't believe I would have been strong enough. We all have different tolerance levels and for us personally, growing up, we were not taught to take a pill for every pain we encountered. That was also true during the healing from my surgeries. At the beginning of the recovery process, the pain was so severe that I had requested medication. The doctors tried many different kinds, including morphine, but none seemed to work. So after a few doses I just gave up on them, and eventually, I built a higher tolerance level. In retrospect, perhaps these surgeries took me through boot camp for what would eventually come down on us years later. And like the toll that surgery and chronic pain can have on a person, grieving can leave you feeling debilitated, exhausted, mentally drained, and even incapacitated. The stress levels are extreme, and the anxiety can tighten muscles in your body that you never noticed before.

It amazes me that in the midst of all the evil in this world, there are so many more kindhearted people. At one of the support groups that I attend, I met a young woman who lost a sibling. She understands the physical effects of mourning; she used her talent as a massage therapist to help others by offering massages to the group members. She talked about the strain and tension we carry on a daily basis and explained that a hot bubble bath or a massage can help make us feel better, possibly even allowing us to heal faster.

I see mourning the loss of a child as living with chronic pain. It doesn't leave you no matter how hard you try; it consumes your thoughts and even your dreams. This can leave you exhausted due to the relentless focus, attention, and energy that are used during the grieving process. The journey towards healing is a slow one. Shortcuts or detours only delay the pain. Sometimes you will feel like you are moving backwards instead of forward, but that is normal. It's important to understand that so when it happens, you won't get discouraged.

It is hard to believe that so much time has passed since my son

was taken from us. Our journey has been long and painful; the pain has lessened and the crying slowly subsided, but I still think of him daily, and I want to believe that I always will. I still find myself praying for him just as I did before and also do for my other kids—I wouldn't have it any other way. The fact that he died doesn't diminish the reality that he is still a very big part of my life.

Early on, I envied families that had not been touched by such tragedy. I would ask myself if this was something for which God was punishing me. I wondered what God was trying to teach me through this. Though I lost my fear of death, I became dreadfully afraid of losing another child. Did I do everything within my power to fulfill their needs, to help them accomplish their dreams? I decided to change whatever I needed to in order to become a better person, parent, wife, and Christian.

The day after Sergio was killed, one of his friends brought over some things he had left at her place, and among those was a small picture frame. But before I saw whose picture it was, she said, "I wanted to bring this to you because I'm sure it will mean a lot to you. I had given Sergio a picture of my daughter," she explained, "but he took that picture out and replaced it with a photo of you that he had been carrying in his wallet. He kept that framed picture of you by his nightstand." Hearing that made me weep of course, but it also touched my heart to know that I meant that much to him.

Just recently, my brother Art shared with me that he was very grieved when Sergio was killed; he told me that Sergio was more than a nephew to him. "He was my best friend," he said. Art told me that Sergio would say that he knew I loved him and this also meant a lot to me. I often wonder what his last thoughts were. Did he reach out to God? Did he know that he was dying? And even in that last moment—when his consciousness was fading—did he feel my love?

Closing Thought

"It's not about how broken I am, but rather what I choose to do with the pieces that matters."

Chapter Nine

SOUL WHISPERS

Dreams—I'm told our loved ones visit us in our dreams. Although not often enough, we cling to these dreams as if they were our lifelines to survival; they keep us going and inject a bit of comfort into our soul. Nightmares, however, are just as powerful as the good dreams and can impact our lives negatively if we let them. What are these nightmares- could they be an extension of our grief? Are they our deepest fears manifesting themselves in darkness— taunting us through our subconscious—in a realm we have no control over? Whatever they are, they can be cruel and leave a lasting effect that can hinder the progress we may be making in our healing journey.

I felt that my nightmares were encounters, during which my soul came face-to-face with insanity, and it was terrifying; it was like a glimpse into hell! After a few of those initial nightmares, my husband began to pray with me, and at one point he began to remind me of the power that is in the name of Jesus. He told me to call on the name of Jesus while in my nightmare. This of course, took some training and practice, plus a lot of prayer but I did my best to follow his advice. As usual, I would pray before I went to bed, but I also included specific prayer for God's intervention with these nightmares and, indeed, as I encountered these regular nightmares I began to learn to speak the name of Jesus out loud in my dreams. I would repeat it over and over until somehow my subconscious would connect with my consciousness and eventually, I would hear myself speaking the name of Jesus and it would immediately wake me up. That helped me significantly. The issue from that point forward was remembering to call on Jesus before my nightmare progressed. Fortunately, the times I was not able to wake myself, my husband would hear me as I was having these nightmares and would wake me up—helping to dispel the evil in my dreams—and he still does.

On one occasion, I experienced a really bad nightmare where I found my son laying on a metal bed at what appeared to be the morgue, just the way I had seen him at the morgue the day after he died. But in my dream he was dressed in a prison jumpsuit and was in shackles. He arose from the bed and looked at me with disappointment and a look that seemed to ask if I blamed him for the altercation that ultimately took his life. I vividly remember looking into his eyes and shaking my head to let him know that I did not blame him for anything, but was, in fact, proud of him for doing the right thing despite how much it hurts to have lost him. I told him that I loved him but he turned away with a hurt look in his eyes, and then he was escorted out of the room—leaving behind, the sound of the chains dragging as he slowly walked away. As I called out to him I began to cry desperately until I woke up to the sound of my own sobbing. I sat at the edge of the bed and cried for a while, feeling utterly destroyed. I found myself clinging to my faith ever so strongly, needing comfort and God's peace. I never wanted to question God, but in my despair, I called out to God and said, "I will not question You, oh God, even in this I will not ask why You would allow my son to be killed. Or ask You why him, why now…why like that? I will not seek vengeance, but I will ask that You show him all that You said You would during that last conversation I had with him; that You, oh Lord will give him all the peace and joy and more love than even I am capable of giving him. And for us Lord, I beg that You help us through this agony, that You carry us in the darkest times—in those times when we feel faint and can endure no more." It was then that I realized that if our days

In my despair, I called out to God and said, "I will not question You, oh God, even in this I will not ask why You would allow my son to be killed. Or ask You why *him*, why now...why like that?"

are numbered, then this would not only be another day of hell but it also meant it was one day less of this life on earth; another day subtracted from whatever that appointed number is, and somehow that gave me comfort…I repeated that in my mind throughout the day… it's one day less, one day closer to the day I can see him again.

I was so heavy-hearted and felt I just didn't have the strength to get through another day of this anguish, yet another long day of suffering. I questioned how I would find the strength to make it through the day to help my other kids get by and do what needed to be done for them…and put on a smile for them, which they very much deserved.

A few weeks later, I had a good dream of Sergio; we were by a river and I was washing his white t-shirt that was covered in blood. I remember that he approached me and I was so glad to see him, yet sad that this blood-soaked garment certainly must have come from his injury. I asked him how he was and he replied that he was fine, and then he smiled. I went to hug him, but woke up before I was able to. When I woke up, I was glad that I'd had this dream, but saddened at the same time since I was not able to hold him; and oh, how I'd been longing to hold him. Later that morning I told my husband about the dream and I cried as I attempted to describe it; I told him that I couldn't understand why in all my dreams and nightmares, I had not been able to hold him. He said to me that perhaps it was because Sergio is now in the spirit and I am still in the flesh, that perhaps the two cannot be combined until I am ready to see him in that light. It made a lot of sense to me and somehow made me feel a bit better thinking that it wasn't because God may have been punishing me or something like that. A few days later, I had the same dream again, but that time he was the one washing the t-shirt and I approached him and told him, "Here sweetheart, let me wash it for you." I started washing it and scrubbing the blood-stained shirt against a rock in the river and as I rinsed it the stains begin to fade away. I sensed that Sergio felt my sorrow and he leaned towards me and said, "You know mom, you shouldn't worry so much about me." There was peace in his voice, and it warmed my heart to hear him say that. The next day I told my husband about the dream. "The shirt you were washing was Sergio, the stains were his sins, the water was the blood of Jesus, and the rock was the Lord," he explained. It gave me chills when I heard him say that, and peace filled my heart that day. Our heavenly Father washes our sins and makes us white as snow; our sins fade as we repent and our Lord forgives us.

A couple of months after his death, I had yet another nightmare; this time it would bring incredible pain and actually cause me to regress in my grieving progress. This dream was a reenactment of the funeral. It became very clear to me that while I was able to keep my composure at the real funeral, and was able to deliver the eulogy, that eventually, my grieving and devastation would manifest itself one way or another—there would be no escaping that. I saw that I could only suppress my grieving for so long before my body and mind would come face-to-face with the magnitude of the reality that my son had been killed. I know that God spared me that devastation on the day of the funeral, but I also learned that I still had to suffer, even if it was months later. I would not be allowed to escape that painful moment because it is indeed also part of the grieving journey.

I remember shortly after the killer was arrested, his allies began their intimidation ploys. Phone calls filled with hate speech, sarcasm, vulgar language, and cruel references to my son's death became unbearable. We went to the police and upon their suggestion we

bought a recording device and were told that as long as we told them they were being recorded at the beginning of the conversation, we would be legally protected. Following their advice, we were able to get a couple of those calls on tape and we turned them into the police; why those recordings were not mentioned by the assistant district attorney during the trial, I will never know, but in one of those phone calls, I could hear the killer's niece say, "I am sitting next to your son's grave. He is sticking his hand out of the grave and in his hand is the knife that he pulled out of his own chest…remember, the knife he was killed with?" I know how stupid that person was for making that call and I know better than to let something like this get the better of me. The truth is that the call affected me deeply because it touched on the pain I felt over the fact that my son did in fact pull the knife out himself. Somehow these people knew about that. I don't remember if I even bothered to reply to her words, but I do remember that I left the room and sat in my room and cried, not only from sadness but also from anger and frustration. This affected me so much because I am still unable to understand the depth of their evilness.

Five years after that phone call and long after the homicide and trial, I had one of the most horrible dreams yet. I dreamed that the killer had taken Sergio from his grave and decapitated his body (I don't want to get into too much detail because it was simply too gruesome to explain). I was made aware of this vile act by the cemetery caretakers, and I found myself sobbing uncontrollably in my dream. I saw his body and face, and I screamed in great anguish and bent down to hold him. I woke up when I heard myself crying. It took me awhile to figure out if this was real or just a nightmare. I say "just a nightmare" very carefully because these incidents cause the same emotional distress as real life occurrences.

God had a purpose for giving me the peace that I needed on the day of the funeral because there was a message that He needed delivered. Now I was feeling all of the raw emotions that I had been sheltered from during my son's funeral. For someone that prided herself in articulating thoughts, I found myself trying to find alternate words to minimize the reality of our loss. The crippling pain that cut right through me seemed to be without mercy, yet I know God had a purpose even for that…the beginning of healing. Perhaps before healing can begin, we have to empty ourselves of all of the ugliness that crowds our heart and soul so we can make room for the healing, a slow and long healing process. In my dream, the grief was so intense that I wanted to reach into my chest and rip out my heart so it would stop beating and therefore, stop hurting…just like his did. I woke up sobbing and gasping for air; that anguish remained for a long time. It may have been that I was suppressing the deepest part of my grief with the focus of finding the killer, but I reached a boiling point and my body, mind, and soul could hold it no longer; it finally released the deepest, most intense level of grief that a human being could ever experience. This was hell on Earth in living form, the cruelest type of pain…but even in the midst of it all, I knew that God was with me and I knew that I had to go through this so my soul could begin to heal. I know that I had to cry all that pain out of my heart so that I could make room for God's love, mercy, and grace—only then could He fill me with goodness.

Unfortunately, I was not the only one that struggled with recurring nightmares—we all did. Imagine, if you can, what it's like for a nine-year-old child to live through his brother getting killed, then to have to endure harassing phone calls that he sometimes answered. Or the knowledge of an acquittal…what did that do to his sense of secu-

rity? It is something so horrific that no child should ever have to be subjected to. It is simply unforgiveable for a person to intentionally mess with a child's innocent mind. There is something so special about children, and it is the responsibility of all of us to protect them. To their own detriment, they will have to realize that they must answer to God for that as well, because they have no idea of the horrific nightmares that he had to endure because of their malicious behavior. I will not divulge the details of his nightmares; I will respect his privacy, but I will say that it was an additional layer of sorrow in the aftermath of Sergio's death.

On March 14, I was riding alone in the car when a song came on the radio that reminded me of Sergio. That night, I had a wonderful dream of him. He was about 12 years old and I was watching a music video of him. I remember saying, "I've never seen this video of Sergio." He was playing the trumpet just like he did in real life when he was around that same age, and I thought, "Hey, he's good." I moved over to get a better look at him, and looked straight into his eyes. He felt the weight of my stare and looked back at me. He paused from playing as if even in that pre-recorded video he could feel and see me. I continued looking at him and he played a wrong note because he looked away from his music sheet and lost his train of thought for a moment. As we looked at each other I whispered, "I love you," and he cracked a subtle smile. He continued to play and I noticed that Andy, my niece Annie, and many others were there as well. It was a wonderful dream; one that made me feel good for a few days.

For over eight years I endured many dreams where I was without the ability to hug him, but I am still appreciative for each and every time he has visited me, if only in my dreams. The oscillating tempo of my dreams brought me to a deeper understanding of the power of the subconscious mind, and they provoked in me ways that helped shape my consciousness and the way in which I choose to react and the decisions I made as a result. Good dreams can bring us some comfort and a certain level of joy, but the bad dreams can make us feel like we've lost ground in our grieving journey; sort of like taking two steps back…like a chutes and ladders game, although in real life, we cannot see the whole picture at any particular point during our long journey, we just keep going- we must. Although I may not be able to reach my son now, and though I may not be able to hold him, I sometimes ask God to tell my son how much I love him, to let him know how much I miss him.

Earlier this year, my daughter Jennie and I were talking about Sergio and some of the things we wish we could do over with him. She and I spent the day together and we spoke about some of the good and bad dreams we've had of him; we also talked about our deep regrets and the trivial arguments. At that time a song, "Hurt," by Christina Aguilera, played on the radio. It always brings me to tears as it reminds me of the last argument that I had with Sergio two weeks prior to his death and the way I feel about it now. The lyrics speak to my regrets.

The argument was over something that my sister Lisa had called me about; she told me that Sergio had been rude to Grandma and I simply would not allow that type of behavior. I came down on him harshly as I feared that he would develop the type of deplorable behavior that Lisa and some of the others had gotten comfortable with. It wasn't until after he died that I learned of Lisa's scheme to get him in trouble. I had scolded my son without giving him the opportunity to explain his side of the story, my mistake, my regrettable mis-

take. But I do thank the Lord for allowing me the opportunity to apologize to him, which I did the week before he was killed. He had come home when he learned about his dad's injury. I saw him fixing something to eat in the kitchen; I went up to him and relayed my heartfelt regrets. In his kindness, he said to me, "It's okay, Mom, I know that wasn't like you." For years I resented Lisa for instigating that argument. I learned that she had become upset that Sergio had begun to ask questions about rumors of her lover storing stolen items at Grandma's house, unbeknownst to Grandma. Lisa was in on the shenanigans of stolen property that her lover was stealing from his job, so having Sergio interfere in their plans may have posed a problem for them. Unfortunately, I cannot change the past, but I can change the present and work towards a better future with my other kids

I may never get answers to all the questions I still have. Those are items that still pierce at me sometimes. The doubts, sadness, anger, and grief that creep up at times- all these are covered by God's grace, I continue to bring them to Him and ask Him to carry me through those moments.

Closing Thought

"The oscillating tempo of my dreams brought me to a deeper understanding, and provoked thoughts that helped shape my consciousness."

Chapter Ten

LIVING LIFE BEHIND A MASK

As a child, I used to love to play the "pretend" game that we all loved to play as children. Whether I was playing the role of a teacher with my younger siblings and cousins, or a famous movie star acting on a mock stage with silly costumes; pretending sent us to a fantasy world where we could be what we wanted to be and reach as high as our imaginations took us. Little did I know, however, that my pretending skills from childhood would prove to be invaluable in the days, months, and years following Sergio's death.

Although I honestly tried to be there for my husband and kids, and kept busy with household chores; I felt more like a zombie, living without any desire to participate in any family functions. I was just going through the motions, getting things done, but with little satisfaction or sense of accomplishment, and certainly without being able to connect with others. I thought I was doing everything I could to keep going and to stay alive; I thought I was doing okay despite the circumstances. I saw myself pretending as well as I had in my childhood years. I didn't want anyone to see how much pain and sorrow was lying just beneath the surface; that thin layer of skin, shielding my soul from exposure to the crude elements. Although I was there in flesh, my spirit was elsewhere, crushed and broken.

The first year was the most excruciating. My first Mother's Day without Sergio was just a week after he was buried and it was simply horrid. I went to the cemetery early that day, before anyone else woke up so they wouldn't notice that I was gone. I lay next to his headstone and began to cry out loud, hurting so intensely . . . as if my spirit was aching all over, crying from the inside out. Dragging myself from his side, I headed home and mustered all my courage to make it through the day. It was a struggle for all of us. I don't even remember if I called my own mother that day or not.

I held back my tears as the kids lit fireworks on the 4th of July, remembering how much Sergio loved the very loud ones. The first Thanksgiving was probably the worst of all of the holidays that year, particularly because traditionally we sit at the dinner table together and after saying grace, we go around the table and say what it is that we each are thankful for. When it came to the part of the table where Sergio's empty chair sat I was screaming inside, and wanted to run. I was tormented by memories of previous Thanksgiving dinners, particularly the year where we had joked about a silly incident that left him without a date. There was laughter then…but only pain and sorrow now.

His next birthday marked a painful milestone. On his last one we had given him the choice of money or a birthday party. He chose the money because he wanted to buy a small car. I had asked him to wait until he finished school and we would get him a nicer car, but being the impatient young man that he was, he decided to buy the one he had set his sights on. This birthday was supposed to be the year that we would've bought his car.

The day before his birthday there were thunderstorms with damaging winds. It was as if nature was manifesting what I was feeling inside. "Quite appropriate for my emotional state of mind," I thought. On his birthday, my husband and I drove to the cemetery to be with our son. We can't say, "Happy birthday!" to him ever again.

We can't hug him and kiss him- we can't even see him. As we arrived at his graveside, we were surprised to see that his brother, Andy, had already been there, leaving behind a white rose with a note attached that read, "I miss you bro. I will always love you." His best friend, Jesse had also visited and left his white gloves, those he had used at the funeral as a pallbearer. Jesse and Sergio were like brothers and to this day, Jesse has never forgotten Sergio's birthday. I have kept the gifts that people have left there for him, and add them to the items that I've saved over the years. We stayed at the cemetery for a while, and we were pleased to see that others had come to join us on this special, but difficult day. Without asking, we were joined by several people including Annie, Daniel, Maribel, Ernie, Veronica, Mario, Juvenal, and Jennie; among others. I remember there was an awkward pause; I suppose this would've been the moment when you would normally bring out the cake and blow out the candles. My husband and I tried to make everyone feel better and we touched his headstone and said, "We love you Sergio." Then I quietly said, "May God celebrate your birthday now in heaven. You have two birthdates now, your earthly one and the date you went to heaven...your angel date."

We, as bereaved parents, cope with our grief as best we can, but sometimes we still struggle even after many years. I still struggle to say, "The anniversary of his death," as do many other parents; and so we say their "angel date." That is the day they went to be with the Lord. Some like to think it's the day they became angels, while others think of it as the day they went to be with the angels.

As I sat at his graveside, I wondered how I would ever go back to the workforce—how I could be productive if I was so torn and absentminded. I could not focus on any particular project for more than a few minutes without being taken by "the thoughts...the shad-

ows." I was usually reminded of the verse, *"Even though I walk through the valley of the shadow of death, I will fear no evil, for You are with me; Your rod and Your staff, they comfort me"* (Psalm 23:4). Indeed that is exactly what this was like…walking through a valley full of shadows of death; a valley so unfamiliar and painful, so dark and full of deep, frightening trenches filled with muddy swamps and quick sand, dragging me down, always trying to keep me down. The pain associated with losing my son was overwhelming and so undeniably real, I could touch it; I could feel it all around me and sense it even while I slept. However, I took comfort in the latter part of the verse, "I will fear no evil, for you are with me." Though there are many forms of evil; this verse tells me that I am not alone and that I have no reason to fear evil because God is the conqueror, God is in control, just as the rest of this Psalm gives me the hope and encouragement of God's presence in our lives, even in the most horrific circumstances. I had to force myself to repeat these verses, to remember God and reach out to Him persistently.

Yes, I had my family around me, but in my mind that torment was all my own, and it was a constant struggle to remember God's presence and love, to stay focused and sane, and to lean on Him. To take hold of His staff to help lift me when I felt I could go no further. That Psalm had been my favorite for years prior to my son's death, but I had never fully understood the power of its words until now. It has now become my fortress.

Getting back to work was difficult, but I was blessed to meet a kind, patient, and understanding man named Robert, who offered to work with me in my new real estate career. He and his family had been friends and neighbors of ours and their support and kindness through our loss became invaluable. I was determined not to let Robert down, to show my appreciation by doing a good job, despite my rather dismal disposition. I do believe that getting back to work after an adequate period of time was good for me because it forced me to keep my mind off of our situation. Little by little my focus and concentration grew, and eventually, I was able to once again feel productive in the workplace. Interacting with other people was difficult at first because I was a different person now. I had a new perspective about the value of life, and often found myself frustrated at the pettiness by some people.

Most days I would cry on my way to work. I tried to control this because I didn't want to show up with swollen eyes. But the memories were not something I could just turn off like a switch. To this day, I try to avoid long trips and commutes; for some reason, while alone in the car, my thoughts will always drift to Sergio.

When I arrived at work, I used makeup to try to hide the swelling but I'm sure that it must have been quite apparent at times.

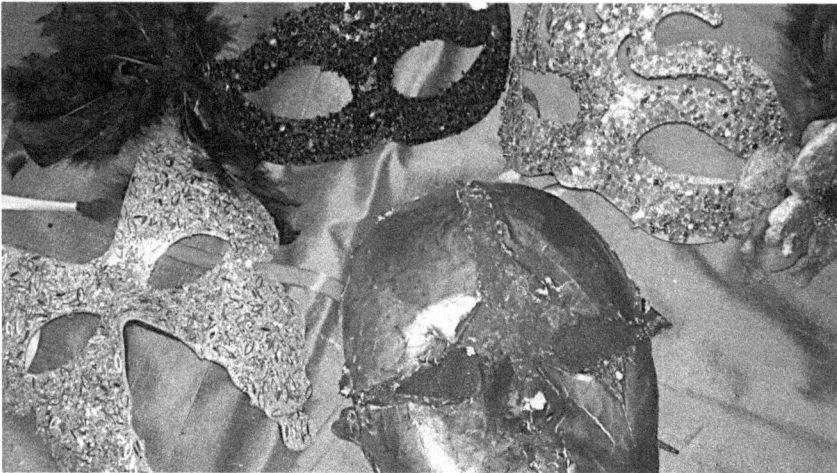

The mask I was living behind was a costume for my game of pretend. I was trying to pretend I was okay but I wasn't—I was crying inside.

One day, I realized that I was living life behind a mask. But this mask was more than a physical, tangible artifact; it was an emotional mask, one that I wore daily to get through the day. The emotional mask was my costume and my acting was from my game of "pretend." These skills were indispensable during that stage of my life. I learned to pretend to be okay, to smile and laugh; all while I was crying inside. Underneath the mask was a little girl, sobbing uncontrollably, hoping to be consoled, hoping to be pulled from that desolate place within me.

Although I thought my true feelings were well hidden behind this mask I had constructed, my kids saw right through it, as if to them, the mask had no effect, to them it was transparent. I began to forget who I really was, and I wondered which one was the real me. Was I forever altered, marked by the homicide that took my son? Was I defined by the tragedy and grief? I was appalled at the notion that I was now a statistic, another victim of gang and domestic violence. What was my true identity, what was I defined by, and how did others see me? Did I even care?

After Sergio's death, I dreaded the thought of holding a job; looking at myself in the mirror as I applied layer after layer of makeup, trying to cover up the traces of tears, tears that just kept flowing. I would think, "This isn't me, this isn't my life." But still, I had to work, even if I had do pretend to be okay; if only to hide the profound pain I carried. However, the mask wasn't enough, my emotions and thoughts wouldn't be so easily covered up. There were times when I struggled not only with the grief, but also with chronic headaches—those days were unbearable.

My challenge was keeping a healthy balance between my grief and my faith. I needed God's strength. Prayer was always in the center of my heart, even in the darkest times—it was prayer and my faith that helped me through the worst times. And because I am human, I feel, I hurt, I grieve; and because I grieve does not mean I lack faith, it does not make me less of a Christian, as some would judge. Healing can come through prayer, but it can also come from grieving. God knows our hearts and he understands our needs and struggles. He, too, had a son that was killed, and I am certain that He wept and grieved when his son was brutally murdered; yet we know that God had a greater purpose and a perfect plan. Unquestionably, it was God, through His unwavering love, that helped me and my family survive this tragedy.

I am happy to say that I no longer live life behind a mask. I decided to take action, to step out in faith, outside my comfort zone, in an effort to help others. This helps take the focus off of me and my pain, and reminds me that I am not the only one suffering and that mine is not the only tragic story. Together, we can help each other along the journey. Helping others helps me heal, it makes me feel blessed, and it gives testimony to the strength we can gain through God when we reach out to Him as we endeavor to fulfill His purpose.

Closing Thought

"A mask may help hide your grief for a period of time;
But don't let it hide who God created you to be."

Chapter Eleven

AT THE CROSS

Driving with my younger kids on the eve of what would have been Sergio's 23rd birthday, I felt depressed at the thought of facing another birthday without him. During this ride, oblivious to the conversation that my kids were engaged in, my thoughts were interrupted by a small voice asking, "Can you see it, Mom?" They went on and on about the spectacular rainbow their innocent eyes were witnessing. At my lack of response, my daughter, Jennie, asked me again and I snapped out of my daze pretending to be aware of what they were discussing. "Well, can you see it, Mom, the rainbow?" she asked. I looked and looked, frustrated that I could not see it for myself, my son pointed in the direction of the rainbow. Finally, I admitted that I could not see any rainbow and my daughter turned to me and said, "That's because you no longer believe." The sound of those words cut deep into the innermost part of me. For years I had taught my children to believe, to have faith, and to never stop dreaming, and now, I was showing them anything but. I had taught them that a rainbow is God's promise that everything will be okay. I felt like I was letting them down. As I tried to concentrate on driving, I thought to myself that I had to get out of that destructive mindset and do whatever I had to do to get back to life...to their life. I resolved to figure out how to survive through the grief in a way that would make my children whole...as much as humanly possible.

That night I had a dream of Sergio; in this episode, I was outdoors somewhere in an area that seemed gloomy and somewhat foggy. I saw myself sitting there…alone, sobbing as I reflected upon Sergio's life and feeling deep sadness over his death. The fog seemed to project a veil that imprinted all the agony I carried in my heart, like a reflection of the misery that was carved into my spirit and the tormented state of my soul. I called out to him, desperately needing to see him. After a few moments, certain I could endure no more, I felt a soft yet strong presence surround me…I noticed him approaching me—dressed in white—and, looking at me with great love and compassion I heard him say "Mom…it's okay." I continued to weep, although this time it was for gratitude and relief, thinking that my son had felt my pain and cared enough to come visit me, perhaps unaware that his presence and kind words would instantly console me.

That night I slept like I had not been able to in months. The first thing I did when I woke up the next morning was journal the dream I had just experienced. Writing that experience down somehow made it even more real and I determined to enter it somewhere just as I saw my misery reflected on that veil, I wanted to sketch the relief I felt as a result of that meaningful dream. I could not stop thinking about that dream, and I was brought to my knees in prayer by the need to draw closer to God. I prayed and I meditated on those things that were tormenting me. I took a deep breath, I searched deep within me, and I determined that I did not want to live with that miserable torment any longer. I decided to surrender my all to God, to bring my anger and torment and leave it at the Cross. I called on God for fortitude to live life—if only for my other kids—but hoping that I would find healing along the way.

I made the choice to renew my faith in God and take Him at His word. These Scriptures from Isaiah encouraged me greatly:

I felt a soft presence surround me . . . I saw Sergio approaching—dressed in white—he looked at me with great love and compassion. "Mom?" I heard him say. "It's okay."

(KJV-Isaiah 41:10), *"Fear thou not; for I am with thee: be not dismayed; for I am thy God: I will strengthen thee; yea, I will help thee; yea, I will uphold thee with the right hand of my righteousness,"* as well as (KJV-Isaiah 40:31), *"But they that wait upon the Lord shall renew their strength; they shall mount up with wings as eagles; they shall run, and not be weary; and they shall walk, and not faint."* This is one of my favorites; it gives me the drive to keep going, reach further, aim higher and soar like the eagles. In fact, it is one of my favorites because it eloquently sums up the promises that empower me to do great things…but it isn't the only reason I favor this one. Every time I read this verse, I recall a conversation I had with Sergio just a few months before he died. We were talking about some people wishing they could be reincarnated into an animal form of their choice; after a long discussion of that theory and the Christian perspective, we both laughed at the stark contrast. He asked me what I would want to come back as, and I jokingly said that I would definitely want to be a lion; you know king of the jungle and top of the food chain…we laughed some more.

When it was his turn to answer, he replied that he would choose to be an eagle; he thoughtfully explained that he admired the eagle's ability to soar high, above all other animals, top of its food chain, yes, but more importantly he said, the eagle, in his opinion, was very much like Christ. His answer caught me by surprise, and I intently listened to his words. I was mesmerized at the beautiful picture he painted with his choice of words, "He can see it all from up above," he explained. I immediately drew the connection and asked if that was the reason that he was always so drawn to the eagles at the different museums we toured throughout the years. He smiled and shared that he was amazed at the span of the wings and the presence they commanded, even behind a glass wall. "But there is something so special about the way they look, their eyes have a sense of such great depth and awe-inspiring insight," he concluded.

I still smile when I remember that conversation and of course, this is the reason that we have come to associate Sergio with the eagle and the lion. The lion not because of what I said but because we think of him as having the courage of a lion, always protecting his family and doing for others; he was our defender.

After entering that dream in my journal, I prayed that God would lighten my affliction. I also prayed for strength, courage, and for great purpose in my life and also for a hedge of protection for our family as I endeavored to fulfill His purpose. I made a vow to Sergio that I would not let his death be in vain, to let his precious memory live on and to repay evil with good. In doing so, I strive to search for noble acts of kindness towards those experiencing the loss of a loved one. Helping them, just as we were helped by so many, allows me to heal inside. I am working hard to let the world know about him, his story, and his character. I want to, as much as possible, live his legacy through my life.

Although the pain remains, we live with the promise that we will see him again in heaven (John 3:16) *"For God so loved the world, that he gave his only begotten Son, that whosoever believeth in him should not perish, but have everlasting life."* I hope that others will be helped through these efforts; that others will come to know of God's strength and let His grace shine for others to see, even in the darkest of times.

Looking back, I ask myself if there is anything I would do differently, and the answer is yes. I was deceived into thinking that happiness was a great career and a bigger house for the family. I was taken by society's notion of success. However, at that final moment, all that mattered to me was my family. I didn't think of the success or the pos-

sessions, all I thought of was more time; I wished and prayed for more time with him so that I could tell him how much I love him one last time. All along I thought I was doing the right thing; you know, what I thought was best for them. If I knew then, what I know now, perhaps things would be different. I learned that we should have a healthy balance between our career and time with our family. Now, to me, success is the proper application of my purpose in life, while placing a priority on my family. My validation will come from the measure of love that I give and that which I receive.

I am fortunate to have a loving family who was there for us and the dear friends who stood by us. The challenges that my family and I have had to overcome have been incredibly painful but we continue to press forward—one day at a time. And along the way, we have made new friends, friends who know exactly what we are going through and understand every aspect of our grief. Sadly though, we also lost a few friends; losing a child has a certain degree of stigma associated with it that some may find too terrifying to deal with. Others have a misplaced fear that it can somehow spread to them, like an infectious disease.

Sometimes even people that have been equipped academically to minister and counsel others can lack compassion and understanding in the area of grief support. At times even our most respected church leaders, well intentioned as they may be, may have no clue as to the level of pain that a human being endures while in mourning. For example, a couple of months after my son's death, I was struggling with the reality that the killer was on the run, and I was overcome with grief; I cried all day. It was a Wednesday night and I felt the need to hear the word of God. I wanted to attend Bible study in the hope of finding comfort. We arrived at the church, my face swollen from crying, but I didn't care, and we found our way into the sanctuary. After a few minutes, I got up to go into the hall where tables had been set up with information about upcoming conferences and retreats. I approached one of the tables to get information about the next women's retreat and was caught by surprise when one of the pastors pulled me aside. I thought that the pastor was going to ask how we were, or, upon noticing the traces of tears on my face, would offer prayer and God's word; instead he looked at me very sternly and said, "Stop it! What are you doing and where is your faith?" My husband and I were shocked and disillusioned that he would say something like that to me, especially when I needed God's comfort the most. I was sorely disappointed and I realized that even some pastors have no idea how to approach a bereaved individual.

I have come to know that I am blessed, despite my son's death. The blessings of my other children remain and I am to focus on them now. At the beginning of our grief journey, however, that was certainly not the way I felt. People would sometimes say to me, "God will bless you," or, "Something good will come out of this." This always seemed so wrong to me. I didn't want a blessing or reward as a result of my son's death! Nothing seemed good to me and I found joy in absolutely nothing. In fact, it took me over two years to be able to say the words "good morning," I would say, "hello" instead; "I'm fine," was replaced with "I'm okay." The worst part was having to say that my son was dead…that word still hurts when I say it. Instead I would say, "He's gone" or "He passed away." Somehow those words seem to ease the blow.

No, the pain is not completely gone, I don't know that it ever will be; but I chose to be well for my kids…all my kids. It isn't that I am utilizing my son's death to gain a reward of some sort—that will never

I go to God daily. His mercy and grace give me strength. I choose to give meaning to the cross I carry; I trust God to deal with the rest. I lay the heavy burden of it all at His feet.

be the case; but it is the need to know that his death was not in vain and the need to do something about it. I want to actively tell his story, with actions, not just words; actions that will show you what he was like, and give you a better interpretation of Sergio's character. It will also illustrate an honest representation of God.

For me, the main source of my strength is God. His mercy and grace give me courage to carry on each and every day. I go to Him daily for renewed strength. I choose to give meaning to the cross I carry, and I have learned that letting go doesn't mean that I have abandoned my son; it simply means I trust God to deal with the rest. I decided to lay it at God's feet, the heavy burden of wanting to know the intricate details of the killer's life, and hoping for justice, which may never come in this lifetime.

My next source of strength comes from my kids and their courageous spirits. They are my heroes and I need them in my life... up front and center.

Closing Thought
"Give meaning to the Cross you carry;
Change the trajectory of your life to honor God."

Chapter Twelve

SIGNS AND WONDERS

Certainly a bereaved individual can appreciate the notion that our loved ones still think of us, far beyond the here and now. But even if you are not bereaved, I hope this section can help enlighten you about a wish that every person who misses his or her loved one thinks of at one point or another: Do they think of us?

Pennies from Heaven

It was during one of the many grief support meetings that I attended where I learned the story of Pennies from Heaven. At this particular meeting, I was handed a penny that had been engraved with the famous poem, which read:

"Today I found a penny,
just lying on the ground.
But it's not just a penny,
this little coin I've found.
Found pennies come from heaven.
That's what my grandpa told me.
He said Angels toss them down.
Oh, how I loved that story.
He said when an Angel misses you;
they toss a penny down,
Sometimes just to cheer you up,
to make a smile out of your frown.

So don't pass by that penny
When you're feeling blue;
It may be a Penny from Heaven
That an Angel's tossed to you."

—Author unknown.

The idea that my son could send me a penny to let me know he's thinking of me, strangely makes me feel comforted, and I can't help but smile every time I see one. When I shared the story with my daughter, Jennie, she too, became interested in the pennies she found. In fact, whenever we are somewhere together and we both see the same penny, we basically tackle each other over it!

I know it may sound silly but when people are in mourning, we cling to whatever brings our loved ones alive. I am certain that people wonder why we would bother to bend down and pick up a penny, but the point is that we need to come to a point where we can begin to do the silly things once again.

One day, a couple of years ago, I was driving to work, struggling with the injustice in the acquittal of Sergio's killer. I became overwhelmed with the fact that the man who killed my son had been set free with nothing on his record. I cried and prayed for strength to battle the anger. I parked my car and continued into work, but I couldn't stop crying. With my head down while walking, I noticed on my right a penny on the sidewalk. I stopped and picked it up. It helped me smile through the pain I was feeling. I continued on and then found two pennies, then three, then I saw a bunch of them. I wept as I felt my son's presence near me and I realized that he sent me those pennies to cheer me up. I picked them up—one by one—and when I finished counting the coins I realized it was the number of weeks since the acquittal. I received a coin for each week, 364 coins total!

I keep those precious pennies in a jar at home and they warm my heart greatly every time I see them.

Actual photo of the pennies that I found on the way into work.

The Butterfly Story

After my son was killed, we moved out of state. Leaving our home was not an easy decision and it came with a hefty price. I had visited my son's grave on a regular basis. Tending to his grave had given me some level of comfort, knowing that I could still take care of him. Moving away hurt and was very difficult.

As the fifth anniversary of his death approached, I asked my husband if it would be okay for us to transfer my son's remains to a cemetery nearby and he agreed, although reluctantly.

I made the arrangements for the transfer and decided on a small ceremony with only a few friends and family. Just a few days before the ceremony, I thought of having butterflies released. However, after the exorbitant transfer fees, I was forced to cut some items off of my wish list, including the butterflies. I was disappointed.

On the day of the transfer and ceremony, my friend Donna took pictures of a butterfly which kept roaming around the burial site. The day after the burial, my husband and I decided to go back to the gravesite to water the plants and I noticed a butterfly that looked just like the one from the day before. I stared at it as it landed right on my son's burial spot. The butterfly remained there flapping its wings—I slowly approached it—fully aware that it could fly away upon noticing me. As I drew closer, I marveled that the butterfly did not move and I reached out and touched it. This large and very beautiful butterfly allowed me to caress its wings for a few moments. I realized I needed a witness to this amazing moment so I whispered to my husband to look. He did and also marveled at what he witnessed. Regrettably, I did not think to ask him to take a picture and capture this little miracle. After my attempt to push my luck and kiss the butterfly, the magnificent creature gracefully flew away, but circled the area before leaving. I was blessed to know that God knew my heart's desire to have butterflies at my son's burial and though I couldn't afford them, God most certainly could, so he sent me a special butterfly, one that likely comforted me in a much more personal way than those I would've bought. Or was it, perhaps, a small gesture from my son, telling me, "Here Mom, I send you this butterfly to let you know that I, too, can tend to your needs and I'm glad to be near you again?" Whatever it was, it was a beautiful gesture, and I will treasure it always!

A few weeks after I saw the butterfly at the cemetery, I met with a group of mothers whose children had also died through tragic circumstances. I had been feeling somber that day and almost changed my mind on attending the meeting. I had been thinking how some people talk about feeling the presence of their deceased loved ones, and I was questioning why I was not able to feel Sergio near me. "Why can't I see you or feel you near me, Sergio?" I asked.

During that meeting we all shared our stories and grief. Halfway through, we took a break, and the hostess sold some postcards she had made for a fundraiser. She handed me one of the cards, and I was shocked when I saw it. On the front was a picture of a butterfly; it looked just like the one I saw at the cemetery. My amazement grew when I read the caption: "you must believe so you can see."

The group leader asked me about my surprised expression; I explained Sergios's butterfly and why I was so taken aback. After a full explanation of the story and its connection to that postcard image, I left the meeting feeling hopeful.

During the long, arduous process of writing this book, I can honestly say that I feel Sergio now, and feel closer to him than ever.

Actual cropped photo of the butterfly taken on the day we transferred my son's grave.

Guardian Angel

Last Christmas season I sent a text to my daughter saying "Jennie, you know how some people think when their children die they become angels, and some even refer to their child's date of death as an 'angel date'?"

To which Jennie replied, "You were the angel first; Sergio thought you were the angel."

"What do you mean?" I asked.

"Sergio looked up to you. You were like his guardian angel. Why do you think he kept your picture by his bed?"

I wept at those words. They touched me deeply. However, I didn't dare tell her what I was thinking—that I could not possibly have been his guardian angel, because I failed to protect him. "Then that would mean that Sergio is a mother's angel and I am an angel's mother!" I said. I don't believe there are biblical references to support that theory, but it's a nice thought.

"You guided Sergio when he was little," Jennie said. "And I believe he is guiding you in this book you're writing and in your journey. I believe that he, along with God, will make of this tragedy a powerful message of faith and finally remove the 'rage' from the word 'tragedy' and work it out for His perfect plan." She reminded me that Sergio was very young and perhaps did not make all the right decisions after I told her that he thought we were trying to mold him into our image. She finished her comments by stating "What do you think he thinks of you now?"

At this, I decided to look up the meaning of the name Sergio. I was really impressed at what I found. My search revealed that the name of Sergio means "Guardian and Defender!" I was amazed at this finding because that is exactly how we all saw him, as a defender.

That it is why we engraved "defender" on his tombstone. It warms my heart to have this revelation confirm what we've believed and said all along. And if this is all true and accurate, then perhaps he may be working as a Guardian Angel now, working on God's behalf in efforts to fulfill a greater purpose.

I also went a little deeper and researched my name and found that the meaning of the name Sandra is "Protector of Man," and "Defender of Humanity." I am not so sure I did a great job to live up to my name in terms of Protector of Man because Sergio was killed, but in the Defender of Humanity, I hope to live up to that part of the name as it relates to the advocacy work I do today; with a relentless passion for justice and restoration.

It is precious little signs and wonders such as these that brighten our days and we value each one because they keep our connection to our loved ones alive. Although I know their spirit lives and those that are saved will dwell in the house of the Lord forever, for a parent, the death of a child is painful nonetheless. I hope that your connection to your loved ones is never broken and that you would recognize the signs when they send them your way... you just have to be willing to believe.

Feeling particularly melancholy one day, I wrote the following:

How I Miss You Child

I think of you in the gentle autumn breeze;

In the most amazing sunsets and the darkest somber settings.

I miss you in the traditional holidays and the private moments of memories created by our

time together and the love we shared.

I ache at the notion of your absence and the distance placed between us;

At the unreachable contact and feel of your hug.

I weep at the thought of your potential viciously robbed and the "what ifs" that taunt me.

I am delighted at the child I loved and proud of the man I adored.

I long for the sound of your voice and the feel of your touch.

I cling to the special bond between a mother and child; and unexplainable tie…the connection of our souls, which transcends far beyond the grave and cannot be severed.

Not here on earth, rather I would much prefer…Oh, that I could spend a day with you in the realm you now reside in, where love and grace surrounds you.

Think of me my sweet as I of you, and know that even in my dreams I long for you.

May the love of God enfold you and may He share with you my heart, and whisper in your ear my treasured sacred thoughts.

—Mom

Closing Thought

"It is precious little signs like these that brighten our days and we value each one because they keep our connection to our loved ones alive."

Chapter Thirteen

SHATTERED LIVES

Immediately after Sergio died, I had great worries of losing my other children. It wasn't only that I dreaded the thought of the assailants hurting another child of mine, or that I imagined that an accident might occur at any given moment, but I also wrestled with the thoughts that caused me to question our own sanity, courage, and strength. I had heard horror stories of individuals that commit suicide after the death of a loved one. This to me was something I regularly forced out of my mind, hoping and praying that Satan could never deceive any of us to the point of such an act. Unfortunately, suicide did hit our home, not my immediate family but my nephew, Angel. His father Raul has been like a brother to me and the loss of his son, for us, is deep and broad. I felt it was important to include his story because it makes me wonder if there was a correlation that may have stemmed from Sergio's homicide; even years later. The perplexing details mentioned in this section may broaden your understanding of the aftermath of violence; or perhaps it's merely a strange coincidence. I would also like to bring awareness to the devastation and profound impact that death by suicide brings to the surviving family and friends.

Angel's Story:

Angel was the youngest of three children in the Villaseñor family. He had two older sisters who nurtured their relationship with love,

care, and attention, which was reciprocated by Angel. He grew up to
be a kind and considerate young man. He was born to my cousin,
Raul, who describes himself as the disciplinarian in the family, always
making it clear that he was his father before his friend; showing his
love for his children with words and actions. While Dolores, Angel's
mom, describes herself as a doting mother that often gave in to her
son's whims. She admits that to a point, Angel displayed some lack of
respect towards her but feels she preferred that friendship be the
stronger part of their relationship. I also spoke to his sisters Yaris and
Edith- they went into great detail regarding the family dynamic. For
clarity purposes, I noted their comments in the Siblings chapter of the
book.

Angel was on his way to completing an associate's degree- his life
was filled with accomplishments in sports, academia, and physical
training. Although a bit of a procrastinator, he exuded a gregarious
personality and had a long list of friends to prove it. Angel often
spoke of his hopes and dreams with anyone willing to listen. His days
were filled with joy, and his life was jam-packed with ambitions for a
happy and fulfilling existence. Longevity however, would prove to be
elusive. The night of May 23rd would mark the darkest day in the life
of this family. It completely shattered their lives and instantly caused
their entire universe to crumble.

As Raul and Dolores prepared to end their hectic day by enjoying
an evening TV show, Angel, at the young age of 21, tragically ended
his life. His parents were right in the next room, completely oblivious
to what was going on inside that bedroom. Unaware of what troubled
Angel's mind, or of the depth of his hopelessness, they didn't realize
that Angel thought that dying—though senseless—must have seemed
like the only way out for him. Indeed parents sometimes sense a

strong need to reach out to their child, but like us, that need tragically may not always manifest itself in time to save a child's life.

At the sound of what seemed like weights hitting the ground, although not out of the ordinary because Angel trained with weights, his dad Raul decided to have his niece Kenzee check on Angel. A few minutes later, Raul heard Kenzee scream; he ran to his son's room only to find him hanging in the closet of his room. Horrified by the sight, Raul immediately began to panic and scream for help as he took his son down and began to do CPR. Dolores quickly entered the room and was confused by the commotion; she heard the panicked tone in her husband's voice as he urgently told her to call 911 and to help him perform CPR on Angel. After what seemed like an eternity, the paramedics arrived at the scene and took over the efforts to resuscitate Angel, though dreadfully to no avail. By that time, his sister Edith had been notified over the phone by Kenzee, who was actually the first one to find Angel. Kenzee told Edith, "Angel hung himself." At hearing such horrid words, Edith's reply was "Shut up!" Hanging up the phone and then hurrying to her parent's house. She explained that she was not willing to accept that the words she heard could possibly be true and was not able to comprehend such a horrid thing. Edith was able to be at the scene before the paramedics transported Angel to the hospital. Yes, Edith was there when those painful words were spoken, "We did all we could, but he didn't make it." She was there to witness when her parents were given the death notification. Still crazed, Edith called her older sister, Yaris who lived across the country at the time. After several attempts to reach her she was finally able to connect and share the devastating news.

A family's life suddenly comes to a screeching halt. Shock, panic, and torment begins to fill the minds of the loved ones left behind, left

to cope with an irrational and drastic decision that would change everything and would bring a lifetime of pain, sorrow, guilt, and anger. A lifetime of confusion over not knowing what went wrong. By all accounts, those who knew him, stated that there were no red flags, no signs of depression or isolation. They will always wonder, "What really happened?" They will struggle wondering if it was a prank gone wrong or an intentional suicide. As a family struggles to survive such a horrific death, they are forced to reconsider their entire life and the decisions they made along the way; they are tormented by the guilt of not being able to foresee his needs—whatever they were—and help save his life.

We were notified about Angel's death immediately. My brother tried to call me and left a tactful message, and then my sister called me a few hours after that. I was distraught, not just for my own pain, reliving the loss of my son, but also because I knew the pain that my cousin, his wife, and their daughters were going through. I knew their confusion, their dismay, their love for their beloved Angel, and I knew the tumultuous road that lay ahead of them. I was brokenhearted because now, others would come to know the level of our pain in a way that only they could understand. I hurt for them knowing of all the anguish their souls would have to endure. I knew what trials and tribulations awaited them at every stage of their journey. Although suicide carries its own set of challenges, the pain is the same, the loss is the same, and the reality is the same…we both lost our 21-year-old boys…they have died, and we are left behind to suffer. Different circumstances, yes, but the tragic death of a child nonetheless. Children we raised, cared for, disciplined, and loved, and in whose lives we placed our hopes and dreams of a better life for them; sacrifices willingly made so their livelihoods would be less difficult. It is a loss so deep that only another bereaved parent can truly understand and relate to.

From the moment I heard about Angel's death, I wondered if my son's death caused lasting damage on Angel- trickle down effects that would manifest years later, along with a multitude of other challenges that family members have had to suffer through. Precarious situations such as these alter the lives of many, and we may not always be able to see the long-lasting effects that may be hiding just beneath the surface. As I mourned Angel's death and thought about the birth and death dates of both Sergio and Angel, I got goose bumps as I realized they were both 21 years old—exactly 21 years old— except for one day off caused by a leap year during the seven years from my son's death. So they were both 21 years and 105 days old, minus one day for leap year.

Weeks later Yaris called me and told me that she had a letter she wanted to share with me. It was a letter that Angel wrote for one of his last courses in college a few months before he died. With her permission, I would like to share it with you.

Overcoming My Fear

I see the meaning of "being alone" as having another meaning than the one that people normally see. Most people see the meaning of being alone as having the house to themselves or not being able to drive in the carpool lane. The meaning of being alone in my eyes is more of a feeling, the feeling of not having anyone to love, anyone to rely on, and no one to comfort you in a time of need. This is my absolute fear. My whole life I always have been surrounded by loved ones who have always been there for me, from the worst moments in life to the greatest. I know that I can overcome this fear through the support that has been provided by my friends and family.

Till this day, I can still recall the day that I started first grade; a little chubby kid, hair combed to one side, wearing navy blue pants with a white-collared shirt. My first day, I was kicking and screaming, holding on to my mother's leg telling her not to leave me there at school alone. Not knowing how school would be, I was a scared boy, with no confidence, so it was hard to make friends. A few days passed, and I started to come out of my shell, I stopped being timid and began to make friends. With these friends I made, I felt safe. I wasn't scared to leave my mother because I knew she would always be there for me when I was done with school. Knowing that my mother would always be there for me and having these new friends, I was content and happy, I wasn't scared being alone any-more.

Still this feeling of being alone haunts me. At the age of thirteen I had a life-chang-

ing moment. To this day I still remember being so alone, and scared. I heard that my best friend, my cousin Sergio got his life taken away. I was devastated, heartbroken and so lost during this time, my life felt like chaos. The person that was so important to me was gone. I felt like I was on my own. I didn't know what to do. Everyone in my family was going through this tough tragedy but the person that I saw that was the strongest through this whole situation was my cousin's mom, my Aunt Sandra. She saw me crying and she knew that I was hurting; and she told me, "Mijo[1], I know that you are in pain. We all are, but know this, he will always be in your heart, you'll never be alone." Knowing that my family is strong has made me realize that I must be strong as well. My family is always there for each other and knowing that my family will always be here for me; being alone is impossible.

This feeling of being alone is the worst feeling that I ever had. That exact feeling is my fear. I still haven't overcome this fear of being alone, but I have learned to cope with it. Every day in my life I think about a situation where people may not love, rely, or be there to comfort me, but having my loved ones

beside me, allows me to remember that, that
isn't true. I know that I can't have someone
there for me every day of my life physically
but I know I will always carry them in my
heart. Knowing this has made me a stronger
individual. As my life goes on, I wish to find
those loved ones that will always be there for
me and share our good and bad moments;
that I will never forget, so I won't be alone.

—*Angel N. Villaseñor*

Living out of the area made it difficult for us to get to the funeral, but I was thankful that they agreed to visit us a couple of months later, when we could share more closely and away from the rest of the crowd. This was a blessing to us because we felt we could offer them some physical distance from their trauma. We felt an even closer connection to them because sadly, we now related to each other on another level caused by the death of our sons. We humbly offered what we have learned in our grieving journey and the things that have helped us along the way.

Like them, family has been the most important aspect of it and the support groups have given us additional resources to help us along the way. We also shared our faith and highlighted the importance of it in our life; the existential crisis that we have experienced and the blessings of God's grace, love, and strength which have made the difference between merely surviving and actually living. The day before they headed home, we invited them to attend a church service with us. My cousin talked about liking the message he had heard during the service. He commented about one of the worship leaders having things in common with Angel; he began to cry and the rest of us along with him. He sobbed as he said, "Sandra, I know you have gone through a lot too, and I know how much it hurts, but this is different," he explained as tactfully as he could, "you have the killer to blame, but who do I blame?" I knew what he was trying to say, as I understood his pain. I tried to console him as best I could by explaining that it is Satan that he can blame, for it was Satan that deceived Angel. Whether it was a prank gone wrong or not, it was Satan that manipulated Angel's will.

That night I pondered my cousin's words as I lay in bed, unable to sleep, "What good does it do me to have a killer to blame? What good does it do me to know who killed my son if I can't go kill him myself because I am bound by morals and spiritual convictions? It doesn't do me any good to know that the man that killed my son is a free man, that he got away with killing my son…it hurts just the same," I thought.

As I prepared myself to write the last few chapters of this book, I wanted to be sure to highlight the similarities in the pain associated with losing a loved one through both homicide and suicide. Although the circumstances are different, both are tragic, both are final, and both leave unfathomable levels of pain. I feel that both of our families have since gained an understanding worth mentioning, which is that the loss of a child is devastating, regardless of the circumstances.

Fourteen months after Angel's death, I sat for a heartbreaking interview with the immediate family and I found validation to my point, that regardless of the type of death, our pain was strikingly similar because we lost someone that meant the world to us and that special someone will forever be loved and missed. The interview also gave me insight into the different elements that make up the various stages in the grieving process, in terms of which phases are more intense for a suicide case. In this case, they are predominantly guilt and anger.

As I joined them in the privacy of their home and took notes during the interview, knowing that they would relive that horrible day, I braced myself to bear through the emotional interview so that we could stay on task. I am forever grateful that they agreed to share with me some of the most intimate details of their tragedy. Before me sat a man I hardly recognized because of the new reflection and demeanor in which he carries himself, a man frail and broken…not at all the strong and rough man I grew up with. His wife was sitting next to me, a different woman, a mom shaken to her core by the debilitating anguish of losing her son; a person, now fragile and insecure, contrary to the bold and boisterous person she once was. Yes, something inside you changes forever, your life changes, your perspectives and priorities become altered, your spirit becomes vulnerable and frail. You evolve into something unfamiliar to yourself and those around you.

I asked the parents what their first reaction was when they saw their son dying and Raul, through tears, explained that it was denial. "It was just not happening, something happened, but not death. I lost control of my emotions," he said. Dazed with what he described as severe pain in his heart and in his mind with a choking feeling he had from his mouth all the way down his throat, a paralyzing type of pain that stayed with him for a long time. There were some people there to offer support but he explained that he didn't want to see anyone because he hated to have to retell the story over and over again to everyone who was asking. This still bothers me because people can't seem to grasp the idea of respecting someone's grief, particularly at the onset. It is not appropriate to put the immediate family through the third degree when facing such a crisis. Unless the family offers to share or asks to be heard, then please do the decent thing and avoid giving the family the added grief of putting them through inquisitive questioning. It will not make any difference in the situation, and the police will conduct a much more thorough investigation. Let the natural progression be of genuine compassion for the victims and their family. It's natural to want to know what happened but please put the needs of the family first- you will know eventually anyway.

Now, getting back to the interview, when I asked Dolores what her initial state of mind was, she replied as she nervously folded a napkin on her lap and struggled through her tears, "I was confused and I didn't know what was going on or why Raul was screaming like that, I didn't know why Angel was on the floor and why I needed to call for help. Then when I realized what happened, I was in shock and then in denial that this could happen." When I asked what the top five grief stages have been for them during this first year, Raul explained that he struggled with the guilt of not being able to save his son when he found him. He drew a picture for us that conveyed his thoughts, "I should've checked sooner and I may have saved him. Now a year later, some days you feel okay and others you feel really, really bad, but the bad ones are not as constant as in the beginning," he said. "But the guilt, I don't think that will ever go away, and I don't know how to relieve that emotion," he admitted.

Dolores on the other hand says she struggles with anger. At my question, she looked down at her lap and began to fold the napkin once again, but not willing to make eye contact as she softly explained that for her it was the anger. "The anger towards Angel for doing this, then anger towards God for letting him go through with it, then anger with myself for not seeing any warning signs, and then anger at Angel again because he never came to me, he didn't talk to me about it and he never gave me a chance to help him."

I asked what their number one regret was, and Raul explained that as a dad he should have had better communication with his son, and then perhaps Angel would have shared whatever he was struggling with. Mom's biggest regret is not being able to identify the danger and wonders if it would've even been possible to know what Angel had planned. "There were no signs of depression or trouble in any area of his life, other than the seldom issues with girlfriends," She explained.

I then moved into the area of their healing journey and asked if they had found any support and comfort during this first year. Raul explained that while he appreciates the generous support they have received from family and friends and by the knowledge they have gained from support groups, but says he has not found comfort yet. He bluntly says that he actually thinks he feels worse now because after the year has passed he has come to realize that this is not a nightmare, that this is real. He does emphasize that the support from their daughters is making the biggest difference, and he points out that "The one day since Angel died that I did feel a little bit of hope was the day that my newest grandson was born; being at the delivery and seeing a new life born gave me hope. Having my daughters and grandkids gives me a reason to survive." Raul admits it's still very hard to look at the dates engraved on his son's tombstone. Dolores also agrees that she feels worse now because she sees the evidence of her son's death every time she goes to the cemetery, and realizes that he will never come back. At first, she says she was paranoid that something tragic might happen to her daughters. She could not bear the thought of losing another child and was not able to sleep. She said that fear has eased up and she states that she would find comfort if she could see joy in her daughters' lives again. She agrees with her husband that their children and grandchildren are their reason for living.

I proceeded to ask if anyone had been struggling with nightmares. Raul said, "I don't have nightmares about seeing him the way I found him. I had one dream of him where he told me he wanted to come home; it's the daydreams that bother me...those are typically about that horrible day when Angel died." Dolores explained that she has experienced nightmares, not of Angel or the way he died, but about her own fears.

Me: If you could spend one day with Angel, would you choose to have him come here and spend it with you, or would you want to spend it with him in his new realm, and what would be the first thing you would say to him?

Raul (Dad): *I would want him to come here, to the day before he died. I would try to make him aware of the pain we feel, which is caused by his death. But I thought I had done that when I talked to him during the funeral of a friend's son who was killed three months prior. I pointed out to Angel how much pain the family was in, and I told him of the suffering that the family was going through. I don't know, maybe he wanted attention, too. If I could see him again, I would say, "I love you."*

Dolores (Mom): *I would want to visit him where he is, to make sure that he is okay there. I would tell him, "I love you. Never forget that I love you."*

---

[1] The word "mijo" means son, but is often used as a term of endearment

In Loving Memory of Angel Noe Villaseñor

A Father's Closing Thought

"The pain that we experienced on that horrible day,
we don't wish it on others."

Chapter Fourteen

SIBLINGS HAVE A VOICE

Giving siblings an opportunity to express their grief and sorrow is just as important as it is for the parents. Theirs is a loss that is deep and just as real. The relationship and closeness they have with their siblings is different for everyone but for those who have a close and loving relationship with their siblings, the pain that comes from losing their brother or sister is profound and devastating. My daughter Jennie brought me to the understanding that when we don't include them in the entire process, they can sometimes feel as if their grief is insignificant and their struggle to survive made to be inconsequential. We must realize that their loss may in fact be deeper than that of a parent because at times these sibling relationships are weaved with other ties that may not be so for the relationship between a parent and child.

Such ties can go beyond the blood related aspect of their relationship; it can also include a deep friendship, a confidante, a role model, a mentor, protectors, and yes, even partners when it comes to mischief.

In this chapter, I have brought back some of the information from the previous chapter, "Shattered Lives," in an effort to separate the story to reflect the parents' perspective to that of the siblings. Just as any other bereaved individual, some people are more willing to share than others.

I begin with Angel's siblings Yaris and Edith. They too were present at the interview with their parents, Raul and Dolores and theirs is a story similar to ours in that they hold a priority to family ties and maintain a close and loving relationship with each other.

Edith, Angel's older sister, describes a close relationship with her brother; she talks about the encouragement and advice that both her and her older sister Yaris provided to Angel. She emphasizes the love and support that never went unnoticed, and their unwavering commitment to their family unity which was prevalent in every facet of their lives. Both sisters took on some of the parenting roles at times when mom and dad were working, which adds another level of responsibility to their relationship with Angel. At my inquiry, Edith explained the difference in how the children were treated by their parents in terms of the male versus female aspect that tends to be typical in the Hispanic culture where the males are normally allowed much more freedom while the females have more restrictions imposed on them.

Edith and Yaris both said their brother was as much a friend as he was their brother. They watched over Angel with love, care and attention; making sure his homework was done and encouraging him to be a responsible young man. With her parents in the same room, Edith talked about the disparate treatment between him and the girls; although it was denied when I asked the parents, Edith explained that Angel was basically allowed to do whatever he wanted, and it was the the girls who carried the bulk of the responsibilities and chores, while maintaining their parent's high academic standards.

Edith said that her brother would tease her and her sister about making full use of the opportunities that mom and dad provided for them, saying that he did not want to waste them, suggesting that the girls did. Rather than be annoyed with him, Edith said that she

encouraged him to do just that and to secure a good future for himself.

Me: What do you remember from that night Edith?

Edith: *My cousin had phoned saying, "Angel hung himself," Upon my arrival, I was confronted with the reality of a suicide scene that included my brother lying on the floor lifeless. As I entered the room I saw that in their attempts to revive him, the paramedics had administered two adrenaline shots but it was too late; my brother never regained consciousness. Soon after, I witnessed the paramedics give my parents the death notification.*

Yaris: *After being told that my brother had killed himself, my sister told me, "They pronounced him," that was all she had to say to me and I knew he was gone.*

Me: What was your initial reaction?

Edith: *Denial, it was like I went into a controlled mood in order to be strong for my parents, and learning that I was pregnant forced me to be strong. The person we knew him as, the strong and happy guy we witnessed was not this weak person that took his own life. Then it was anger, anger towards Angel, but then I feel really guilty for feeling that way. It's a constant struggle between the anger and the guilt and, oddly enough, I feel selfish for thinking those things, for thinking that I may think too much about my own pain and the deep sadness that still overwhelms me. I feel like I have not grieved yet, like I am suppressing it until a more suitable time, like when my parents are better. I couldn't cry; I was holding it in. I just couldn't do that yet because I was afraid that I wouldn't be able to stop and then I would not be there for my parents.*

Me: What I see is the opposite of selfishness. You have exemplified the love and respect that you, as well as your sister, Yaris have for your parents. I am very proud of the way that you both have sacrificed your own grieving during this horrible loss, and put your parents' needs

ahead of your own. I think that's admirable. But I encourage you to find a way to relieve some of that grief because it's not healthy to suppress it and pretend it's not there; we all need to have our time of mourning and we all need the support from family and friends that can help us get there.

Yaris: *Pain, everything hurt and the tears would come and go. I felt numbness; I got to our parent's home 24 hours after they took my brother's body away, and I was in disbelief. I saw everything just as he left it and all I wanted was to see him walk in the door. I felt immense anger, lots of it for everything that happened, how it happened, anger towards me and the people around Angel at the time.*

Me: What has helped you during this first year?

Edith: *Staying busy with kids and family helps me to not to dwell on it obsessively. The guilt and the anger have eased up, but then again I feel guilty that I may be getting better.*

Me: Personally, I can relate to Edith's words, the mental struggle that we encounter during the grieving journey is one that carries a lot of anguish because the love for our loved ones is so great, that feeling like we are recovering from their death seems wrong somehow, it literally feels like you are letting them go…and that really hurts.

Yaris: *My sister Edith was my help through it all; I feel we were there for each other because we understood each other.*

I continued pressing forward with the questions; as much as I hated to have them relive their torment, I wanted each of them to share and to relieve some of the grief that was bottled up inside. At this point my main concern was that they may have this brief moment to express their anguish.

Me: One year out, have you found any comfort?

Edith: *Not really. I found that some of the support groups have helped in terms of the knowledge I have gained. Suicide prevention is very valuable; to most of the people in the support group sessions the loss of their loved ones came as no surprise, painful yes, but not shocking because the majority of them had experienced depression or psychotic behaviors prior to their suicide. They may take comfort in knowing that they tried to help their loved one, but we didn't even get the chance.*

Yaris: *One year after Angel's death I don't feel any better, every day is a little different but it is still difficult to know that he is not here anymore. I would not say worse, just not better. My friend, Arlene helped guide me through the difficulties at the beginning. She was a true friend in all of it. Family support was offered until we were ready to face it all. Counseling, family therapy, and support groups have helped, and so has the understanding from people experiencing similar stages of grief. It helped to not feel alone in our fears and emotions. Another source of comfort is seeing Angel's friends still come around and visit, they remain in our lives and that makes me feel like a huge part of Angel is still with us. I feel deep sadness, which has taken over our lives; mostly for not being able to be there for Angel, and for my family. I fear not being able to cope and letting the sadness take over. My biggest fear in all this is that I might never understand what exactly led to my brother taking his own life.*

Me: Did you feel the majority of the attention went to your parents?

Edith: *Yes, but I was actually relieved because I knew that my parents needed the help, that this was their child and I saw how devastated they were. My parents needed all the help they could get and having people there for them, gave all of us the added support that we desperately needed.*

Me: Have you suffered from nightmares?

Edith: *No, but daydreams are bad because they always go to that tragic day. I remember I had two dreams, one where I was in disbelief that I was actually seeing him. I went to touch him and kept touching him to make sure he was really there. The other dream was about me telling him that I needed to physically see him and*

he asked me why, and then he told me to just text him.

Yaris: *I have not had nightmares, as a result of his death but I have dreamt him happy, just as I remember him.*

Me: What is your biggest regret?

Edith: *Not calling him the week before, when he told me that he needed me, that I was the closest one to him next to mom. He had some issues with his girlfriend, but I didn't want to meddle or interfere, but I realize now that I should've approached him.*

Yaris: *What I regret most of all is not being there with him that day.*

Me: If you could spend one day with him, would you have him come here or would you chose to go where he is, in his new realm and what would be the first thing you would tell him?

Edith: *I would have Angel come here. I would tell him that I loved him...that I really love him; that this was not the answer, not the solution.*

Yaris: *If I could have one day with Angel, I think I would want to go where he is because I like to think he is happy and peaceful in heaven, and I would want to share that with him. Many times we are so wrapped up in our own lives that we fail to see what is going on around us and we do so little, fearing that it will interfere with that life. I feel that as a family we need to be more comfortable communicating, doing more when it matters. Losing my brother has been the most difficult thing in my life thus far. I know I will always have sadness over losing him like that, but I think the best we could do is to remember him always, and have the peace of mind that we are one day closer to being reunited.*

It was difficult ending the interview with the way they were feeling at that moment, but I had to catch my flight back home. I asked my children if they wanted to contribute any content for the book. It was a difficult decision for them because of how painful this still is. Andy and Jennie did want to share what they wrote for Sergio.

To My Brother

He would not want to see us cry; he would want to see us smile.

He would want us to remember how he lived rather than how he died.

How funny he was; how crazy he was. How he impacted all our lives.

He left his mark on our hearts; he made us all smile, he made us all laugh.

If you were around him for just five minutes, you would know the kind of guy he was.

There was never a dull moment with Sergio; we all have stories to share that could last two lifetimes.

He had a heart of a lion, and was the most straight-forward guy you ever knew.

He would tell you what he thought even if you didn't want to hear it.

I pray to God to let me wake up; that this is all a bad dream and it's not really happening.

I keep waiting for him to walk through that door and that he is fine. But as the days go by, it just gets harder so I began to realize

that I will never see him again; and it's more than I can bear.

He was my brother, your son, and our friend.

We Love You Sergio and we will never forget you.

—Your brother, Andy 2004

A Sister's Message

There was no compassion, neither remorse nor shame. Perhaps that's what makes the killer so wicked, crude, and malicious. A brutal massacre had taken place, a brutal war that we lost in flesh but won in spirit. The very people I thought I trusted turned out to be thieves and vultures, for killing my brother and destroying my life; then feasting away on what was left of me— they are savages.

Sergio, the sound of your voice taunts me like a broken melody of sorrow. If life is sound, then I am deaf; if love is voice, then I am mute. I was unable to grasp what I held dear for so long. There was nothing left for me; nothing but torment and pain. I was overwhelmed with despair, and it was just the beginning, the dawn of wickedness. Torment, turn from me, I say!

The pain and anguish in my eyes will consume me; nightmares became a reality and reality became a nightmare. Spring no longer blooms and the color of in my mother's eyes have become dull...a very sad and pail Spring remains that blends into the dreariness of winter. I was saddened when the flowers wilted, when the cherry blossoms withered away—as a reminder of living things, vibrant organisms that die—leaving us to frown upon their departure, painfully forcing us to tend to the remains.

And I realize it was a very relevant metaphor of life itself; no longer do I feel the warmth of the sun on my shoulders and the sweetest of nectars have lost their taste. Distraught, confused, like a riveting bat in a dark cave not knowing where to turn, not knowing what to do. My eyes began to swell up with terror; I swallowed reality and sensed evil when I tasted death. My life on the brink of insanity and in the midst of it all, I found nothing; nothing but memories filled with malevolent, venomous, and predatory acts. Alas, even justice was taken from us; justice wickedly manipulated and even in that, the killer prevailed.

The bitterness of life has captured me and does not seem to depart from my soul; my spirit tied in sharp, rough shackles, a slave to pain and sorrow; and so, here I dwell, in the chamber of agony, until the rider of the white horse comes to set me free!

Rest in peace my brother...until I see you again in the gates of heaven, where we can be a family once again.

—Your Sis, Jennie Huerta 2005

... here I dwell, in the chamber of agony, until the rider of the white horse comes to set me free!

A Sibling's Closing Thought

"When everyone showed up to offer their condolences, they forgot that I too was grieving. I felt I didn't matter, yet my pain was just as deep."

Chapter Fifteen

REDEMPTION'S LABYRINTH

Have we journeyed far enough on this difficult Path? Have we mended our lives sufficiently so that we can allow our spirits to rest? I say, "no, not yet."

But that is speaking from my own convictions, my personal healing journey my very own life experiences—my redemption's labyrinth.

Walking in this painful journey has led to deep soul searching. It has led to reflecting upon my life and the trajectory that I wish to follow. For a parent, finding redemption from those times we fail our children is a heavy burden and finding redemption from God might seem unattainable. Before I could begin in the path of redemption I had to forgive myself in order to be able to move forward. But sometimes forgiving ourselves is the hardest

We can wander aimlessly in search of redemption but we can get lost. Keep your sights on Heaven.

thing to do. I did not get the opportunity to ask for Sergio's forgiveness before he died, which made it harder for me to forgive myself for my perceived parental failures.

But I had to make peace with myself, with my son, and more importantly with God so that there could be room for restoration. I had to somehow find courage and strength so I leaned on the Lord and fasted while I prayed for forgiveness, peace, and for healing.

Bereaved parents often struggle with the torment of self-condemnation; whether at fault for the death of our child or not, we tend to punish ourselves with relentless thoughts of guilt over past arguments or situations that we now feel we could have handled better. This is particularly true for parents whose children have died by suicide. The incessant thought of, "Why didn't I check sooner?," or "Why didn't I notice there was something wrong?," or "How could I have missed the signs?," all take a cruel and debilitating toll on parents, wearing out the body, spirit, and mind of each affected individual. Every parent goes through this phase no matter how our children died because hindsight is always 20/20. We all think back to those moments where we question our ability to have appropriately disciplined our kids and then we condemn ourselves when we feel we fell short of our own expectations.

This may be one of the most difficult phases to endure because it is not one that will pass by in a few months. In my opinion, the older the child was, the more baggage there is to punish ourselves over and the more opportunities to blame ourselves if we feel we didn't do everything in our power to make sure that our child lived a healthy and happy life. But happiness is what? And how do we measure at what point they could've been at their happiest? What do we use to measure those healthy, happy levels, and at what measure do we then determine that it was enough? But it may never be enough because we are parents and we want nothing but the absolute best for our children, yet we have to be realistic to the limitations placed upon us by our humanness, , by nature, adversaries, and even God himself. God wants us to be dependent upon Him alone and so we must draw our attention to the joy that comes from the Lord. Now we know that happiness and joy are two different things; where happiness can be a temporary, superficial, and even tangible moment; joy on the other hand is everlasting, deep, solid, and made perfect in Christ. In reading the passage below, I recount the numerous moments that provided opportunities for us as parents to instill in our children the love of God in their hearts. A love so deep and real that they would be able to carry it with them and call upon it in their time of need; or sufficiently enough to overflow in their lives as abundant joy made evident by the strength in their character and the blessings in their lives.

Romans 5:1-5 (NKJV) *Therefore, having been justified by faith, we have peace with God through our Lord Jesus Christ, [2] through whom also we have access by faith into this grace in which we stand, and rejoice in hope of the glory of God. [3] And not only that, but we also glory in tribulations, knowing that tribulation produces perseverance; [4] and perseverance, character; and character, hope. [5] Now hope does not disappoint, because the love of God has been poured out in our hearts by the Holy Spirit who was given to us.*

It is a continuous process that requires willful effort to lay our burdens down at God's mercy seat and ask for deliverance so that we may feel forgiven by our loved ones and by God our Father, who has set the best example for parenting. But not only redemption for the times we feel we may have failed our children, but redemption for our own failings with God. Peace will come through this reconciliation

process between God and ourselves so that we may continue on this healing journey and thereby be healthy and productive; this is particularly important if you have other children. Learning to become a better parent for the sake of our surviving children is crucial if we are to redeem our faltering qualities; this will leave less room for future regrets. Our focus now should be to make sure that our surviving children inherit the true blessings of joy, which comes from a strong relationship with the Lord.

Redemption and reconciliation by works can be a slippery slope, because mortals tend to measure their own self-righteousness, which can also be ever-changing and different. Therefore, we must set our compass on the eternal sight and the never-changing God, for He alone is our Redeemer and through Him our eternity sealed by the atonement of Christ.

> (Romans 5:8-11 NKJV) *But God demonstrates His own love toward us, in that while we were still sinners, Christ died for us. [9]Much more then, having now been justified by His blood, we shall be saved from wrath through Him. [10]For if when we were enemies we were reconciled to God through the death of His Son, much more, having been reconciled, we shall be saved by His life. [11]And not only that, but we also rejoice in God through our Lord Jesus Christ, through whom we have now received the reconciliation.*

Before I could even contemplate the thought of redemption, I had to be completely empty in order for God to come in and begin the restoration process so that He could have a clean vessel to work with. But I longed for more, much more than just healing. I needed God as my Redeemer and my Savior; then and only then could I obtain the peace that I had desperately been seeking. I had to find the true essence of God and get an accurate image of Him, not one that would mold to my standards but one that required me to transform to His. I was the one that needed to change, not Him; I was the broken one that needed mending and healing. I think of the crucifixion of Christ and how He had to come to the darkest point in His human life, and then suffer a torturous death followed by a waiting period, before ultimately being rewarded with a glorious resurrection.

I believe in God's purpose behind the crucifixion and I live by the promise of salvation that is given to us as a result of our acceptance of Jesus as our Lord and Savior. But, can you imagine what Mary, his mother, must have gone through to see her son tortured mercilessly while she witnessed with agony as her son—her child—died slowly and painfully? She endured the most unfair trial and horrific murder-all, while Jesus was sinless. Even if Mary had fully known the extent of the purpose behind the sacrifice, the pain of her son's death would be excruciating nonetheless, particularly because of the manner in which he died and the torture and agony that He had to physically endure, which undoubtedly pierced her heart at every blow and for every drop of His precious blood.

Amazingly she survived through unfathomable sorrow and I wonder what thoughts must have crossed her mind. Was it that she should focus on her faith in God, just as she did when she was informed by the angel that she would carry God's child? Is it plausible to consider that she, too, would be tormented by the grief because of her own humanity? I tear up when I think of what joy she must have felt upon His resurrection, she saw her son alive again, knowing that the physical pain He endured and the emotional pain she suffered was just for a brief period in time compared to the promise of eternity. I want to feel that same joy, I want to see my son again and know that there is

a greater purpose than what the killer intended, or that which my mind is limitedly capable of comprehending. I want to feel God's peace, strength, and love as I endure the rest of my life without my child. Thus, I will purpose to bring meaning to the cross I carry and the sorrow that will reside in my heart until we are all reunited again in Heaven.

How can you do that? How can you get from a dark and miserable place where sadness reigns and where the mind has no rest from guilt and regrets? How do you find your way towards the path of restoration and even redemption? It starts with making the decision to survive and having an unwavering determination to not let the death of our loved ones be in vain, and by finding a meaningful purpose that will honor our loved one's memory and bring glory and honor to Christ our Lord. But it doesn't happen overnight and it's important to allow an appropriate time for mourning and grieving. Once we feel well enough and stronger in our journey, we can eventually begin to fill that void inside us that was left by the death of our loved one. Although it may never be filled completely because we will always miss them, God can fill that void with His love through His mercy and grace. It is about stepping outside of ourselves and doing for others. It's about forgoing some of our own personal time for grieving, and then serving sacrificially when the need arises and we are called upon to help pull someone else out of the pit of despair. But not for the sake of performing good deeds, it's about serving the Lord despite our own struggles, and surrendering our will to Him.

This is not a fairy tale book; it does not have a "Happily ever after" ending. I still have a long way to go, I am well aware of that. I need to carefully and respectfully address the issue of reconciling my feelings about the killer with my Christian faith. I am referring to the

Lord's admonition to forgiving and praying for those that harm and hate us. I know that I speak for millions of other parents out there that have lost a child through a violent crime and have never been able to bring themselves to forgiveness; while others have found the grace necessary to come to that place and freely offer it whether it was requested or not. I know what the Bible says on the subject and I believe this is a very intimate and personal topic for every individual. I also believe that God knows our hearts and he understands every thought...even before we think it. It is an extremely difficult subject to touch on—forgiving—wanting or not wanting to forgive them, or even the aspect of whether or not they would want to be forgiven. This area is a layer that I am still working on. It's a part of the number of tiers that are under construction...a work in progress, as am I.

However, I am making great progress as I travel in this journey I am on. I am not free from pain and sorrow, nor do I believe that I will ever be completely but I am determined to keep moving forward and to stay focused on the things that matter. Of course I am years after the death of my son, so the grief is not as intense as it was in the beginning. I am aware that some of the things that I am writing about may seem unbelievable or unattainable if you happen to be at the early stages of your grieving journey; it takes time to get to a more stable step in that journey and believe me it can happen but only if you are willing to get there.

Closing Thought

"Stop wandering and set your compass on the never-changing God,
for He alone is our redeemer and through Him our eternity sealed,
by the atonement of Christ."

Chapter Sixteen

BITTER OR BETTER

I've attended numerous support group meetings and heard many heartbreaking stories from other parents. I have also performed countless hours of research on the death of a child. Some have been destroyed emotionally; others have been destroyed financially, while others have allowed their tragedies to destroy their families or their marriage. I have witnessed the contrast between those that have chosen to be bitter and those that have chosen to be better.

On the topic of the torment that I personally suffered from the shocking acquittal, I have come to the conclusion that a verdict, be what it may, is not necessarily what will make a difference in the grief we carry. I know for a fact that had the killer been convicted, and even if he had received life in prison, it still would not take my pain away. I learned this as I interviewed other parents that have also suffered the death of their children.

I will illustrate three different cases. The first, a mother, and dear friend Lu, whose daughter was murdered a few years ago but that killer has yet to be identified. She lives with the torment of wondering if anyone around her killed her daughter and may very well still be within her circle of friends or family. She wonders every time she talks to any of her daughter's friends or acquaintances; her pain is unimaginable. The second is a grieving mother whom, I visited with and whose son was murdered by gang members who did in fact receive a life sentence yet she is still not very functional because of her grief.

She worries that someday the killer will be given parole; she too was harassed and intimidated by the killer. And third, a father whose young child was killed and cannibalized. The killer was convicted, but the father accepted a plea deal for a 40-year sentence. Now, after a successful appeal, the killer will be released many years earlier than the plea agreed upon. That father is devastated beyond belief. He, like me, feels guilty about the plea. Even though he accepted the deal and that killer did spend some years in prison; on the other hand, I refused the plea and this killer was acquitted. We both have had to live with our decisions and we both have come to regret them.

After putting all this research together I saw the similarity in these cases. The grief is there regardless, the pain level much too intense for the human mind to comprehend—and that is because our child was killed, our child is dead... and there is no changing that. The void that their death leaves has nothing to do with the criminal's sentencing. What a conviction does is bring some relief that the killer will remain behind bars and will be held accountable.

It is easier to become bitter over tragedies that have come our way than it is to choose to be better; because choosing to be better will take serious effort and commitment.

Though I sincerely understand that grieving and mourning can bring on all sorts of emotional phases and that we are all different in the way we cope and grieve, I believe I have experienced most of the grieving stages that we often hear about. I admit that the parallels that exist for many mourners, particularly for those with similar types of death, are real and undeniable and that is why it's important to learn from others. I encourage everyone to reach out for help wherever that help is and in whatever form you need it, as long as they are healthy options with a sensible balance. Allowing yourself to move beyond the current phase is important for many reasons and only you can determine what is best for you in your situation. Although we can all share our own testimonies and highlight the methods that worked best for some of us, it does not mean those same methods will work for everyone. Each person must try different things until they find the method of healing that works best for them.

I have seen how some mourners have chosen destructive paths in dealing with their grief. While we may encounter some intense sorrow, deep anguish, and certain levels of anger, dealing with it in a destructive way may intensify all these emotions and hinder the healing that you so desperately seek. You can isolate those people around you who are willing to help but they may reconsider their level of commitment after a period of time if they believe their efforts are futile. Keep in mind that sometimes the people around you may not know how to deal with the death of a loved one but most are willing to help out in some way or another. There is a lot to learn for both the family and the friends that want to help. Realize that not every mourner has people around them that are willing to offer support, so burning your bridges will only make matters worse in the long run. Although there are times when people can be disingenuous, rude, or insensitive, the fact remains that death is one of the most difficult things we will ever have to deal with and the ripple effects of death are vast and complex.

There are a wide range of peculiar situations we may encounter as a result of our child's death. My own father for example, was insensitive during the most painful time in my life, and the only words he ever said to me during the entire process left me hurting even more. My father had himself experienced the devastation of losing his first-born son and I felt he should have been more compassionate. The day after my son was killed and people began to gather at our home, I

remember weeping as we were sharing some of the details of of Sergio's death but all my father could bring himself to say was, "These things happen." Those words hurt more than he will ever know but I did not respond to his comment because it is not like me to talk back to my parents. Now I admit he has never been a very doting father and has always been a man of few words, nonetheless, this came across as very insensitive. I understand that he may not have been aware of his thoughtlessness and I don't resent him for it.

During a recent trip to California I was able to visit my father and after eight years it affected me to see how debilitated he is. A few years back he'd suffered a stroke and became disabled and is now unable to speak. During this visit I was able to talk to him about God and about things that mattered even if he couldn't answer me, I still felt they needed to be said. I asked if in his heart he was doing okay. He tried to speak but couldn't so I asked him to nod if he meant to say yes... but he didn't nod. I stayed for a while and toward the end of my visit I told him that I love him and I asked if he understood what I was saying. He looked at me and nodded yes, affirming what I had said. I then asked him something I'd longed to hear my entire life. I asked if he loved me too and he looked at me and with tears in his eyes he nodded again, telling me that he did love me. Neither of us had ever spoken those words to each other because we did not have that kind of relationship. In my heart, all these years later, not knowing if I would ever see him again, I felt those words needed to be spoken... and that was that.

The following are things and items I have seen to be destructive and would respectfully suggest that you refrain from doing:

• Don't become vengeful, as this may cross your mind if your child was murdered or killed by accident; whether by a careless or drunk driver, a bad fall, a prank gone wrong, among others. Your family and friends do not deserve another tragedy.

• Don't let it destroy your life even if you have to switch to a new career and change your lifestyle, find a way to keep living.

• Don't let it destroy your family or your marriage. Find ways to work through it together, patiently, giving each other love and respect.

• Do not use their death as an excuse to be offensive or hurtful to others. Don't take it out on those around you. Dealing with a devastating loss can be overwhelming; you must take care of your physical and mental health.

• Don't become a bitter person. You can choose to be bitter or be better. Let go of the hate and anger but don't let go of your loved one's love and the memories that will help keep him or her alive in your mind and in your heart.

• As much as possible, try not to neglect your responsibilities, although in the beginning you may need time and help to get through the most critical stages of your loss; eventually, you have to move toward a new normal and a productive state.

• Do not let the tragedy become your character, empower your life and your course of action. Only you can decide what you will do with all the chaos.

• Do not live your life in a way that would negatively and shamefully represent your loved one; bring honor and reverence to their

memory.

• Do not resort to alcohol or drugs (unless medically prescribed, but be cautious not to form an addiction) as this will only make matters worse, not just for you, but for those around you.

• Do not let guilt and remorse destroy you. Forgive yourself and learn to be at peace with your soul; you would want the same for them. I know this is easier said than done but seek God's forgiveness and peace and He will deliver it to you—perhaps not overnight—but He will.

At one of the support group meetings that my husband and I attended a few months after my son was killed, some of the group members were going on and on about their hate and feelings of revenge. I left that meeting feeling worse than when I walked in, but I left with an understanding that we have a choice and we all have to make a conscientious decision to do what's best for us and our families, and what is best in the eyes of God. It takes a bigger person to do the right thing rather than act out of anger and revenge, even if it were justified. Choose instead to channel that energy into productive options; live a useful and even dynamic life…that's the best revenge.

Closing Thought
"We will encounter intense sorrow, anguish, and anger,
but dealing with it in a destructive way may intensify your grieving
and hinder the healing that you desperately seek."

Chapter Seventeen

BE A SURVIVOR

Let's walk together in a meaningful journey of survival and a constructive revival. Together we can become a society of survivors with a purpose to restore lives and help mend broken spirits. It must be done one step at a time. It begins with the willingness to heal, to progress, and to find ways that make sense for you. This may require that you try different methods of healing until you find the one that works best for you. Pray for guidance, God will help you just as He has helped me. Don't give up. Keep moving forward. Going to church has always been a place of peace and inspiration for me; we have an amazing pastor, whose energy and passion for God transcends to the congregation and you can't help but get motivated. Reading my Bible is another source of inspiration... but my secret is the love I have for my heavenly Father! You will notice the change slowly, but initiative is crucial and must take place from within, honestly and wholeheartedly. Seek the Lord's purpose then focus your energy in that direction. If you knew you could not fall or fail, would you take that leap? If you knew you had a safety net beneath you, how far would you be willing to go? Grow in your relationship with God and let Him be your safety net, your shield, and your Savior. If I can survive my son's death, then I can survive anything…and so can you!

If you have experienced the loss of a loved one, don't put so much pressure on yourself to be everything to everyone for the sake of "being strong." Do what you need to do to get well, even if at times you take some steps back; as long as you make the effort to move forward you will survive. Your priority is to take care of yourself in order to be able to take care of others.

After you feel you have gained enough rest, strength and healing, I would encourage you to step out of your comfort zone and reach out to someone that can help you, and then when you are ready, perhaps you can help others. Don't let the tragedy define you, you have the power to define your choices and your course of action. People that have experienced a similar loss are often willing to help others that are recent in their grief. God sends people to us that have been through similar circumstances so that we can encourage one another.

Remember that everyone grieves differently and each one of us is wired to God's master design. We cannot set certain expectations of others based on our own capabilities—it simply wouldn't be fair— even if you have suffered the loss of a loved one and are now trying to help others, remember that the many different stages of grief hit each one of us at different times, and for varied time periods. For example, I was first hit with the shock and denial phase but that may not have been the same for my husband or for my kids. After the funeral I went through the deep sadness and during the trial, I experienced severe anger combined with all the other symptoms.

For some, it may only be one or two different phases, but they may last longer or be felt more intensely. Newly bereaved individuals should not let others dictate how long a grieving period should last, that, too, varies with each individual. Some people have unrealistic and at times unhealthy expectations of those in the mourning process, particularly if they themselves have not experienced such a loss. Sometimes, in their mind they formulate a mandate of what is acceptable. It is very hurtful to the grieving person to have others try to disrupt whatever progress has been made; it leaves the bereaved feeling uncomfortable and at times wondering if they are normal…and the last thing they need is for some insensitive person—though well intended—tell them it's time to move on. Respectfully, I will say that the loss of a child is like no other. I can personally attest to the greater depth of pain and chaos associated with the loss of a child. This is not meant to belittle the loss of other types of relationships. I have lost other family members as well, and while they have been severely painful, the pain from the loss of a child is unimaginable and can last forever.

Sadly, I know I will never get Sergio back, and no matter what, the emotional scar will always be there to remind me. What once was smooth and living tissue, blissfully ignorant to the possibility of injury became like a deep flesh wound that exposed raw carnage; grotesque, yes, and painfully invisible to the naked eye. A life cut short, with devastation left in its place. In the same way, a bare, deep, and painful emotional wound filled my heart, but the scar tissue was cluttering everything around it, leaving very little room for anything good. And if left untreated, it could become infected. If tended to, however, healing could take place. But it would be a gradual recovery where the wound evolves into a scar, still emotionally present, never completely erased. On the surface you could not imagine how much damage was done, how deep the wound was, how long it took to heal, how well I tended to it. I came to realize how fragile life is and how the human body fights for survival. We are created with an innate need to survive, to recover and live—even when we don't want to. You breathe without effort while you sleep, and you panic when your breathing is interrupted for a prolonged period of time. Your heart beats on its own even if you prefer it didn't. Each beat pumping oxygen and life into

your system, does it not? I believe the human spirit and soul were created similarly. Just as the body can heal itself, so, too, can the soul.

Perhaps you've heard of the philosophical thought experiment, *"If a tree falls in the forest and no one is around to hear it, does it really make a sound?"* Likewise, I would pose a similar question, *"If a person is in torment, but doesn't say a word, is her mind really screaming?"* I dare say yes to both, and because in both instances God is there, He can hear them both, and just as loud. Simply because there is no other person around to witness the episode- it does not mean that it isn't real. If our mind is connected to our soul and our spirit then our body is also connecte but in a outwardly way. So call out to God physically or spiritually, He can hear you just the same. Whether you eloquently articulate a message verbally or scramble to formulate a cohesive thought in your mind, it will all make sense to God.

Don't try to suppress the grief; try to manage it instead. Otherwise, the grief will surface sooner or later. You don't want it to eat away at you internally and poison your life. I will not lie to you; at times the journey may feel like it's leading you through a dark tunnel, especially in the initial stages, weeks or months after the loss. Although in this tunnel you may or may not be able to see the light at the end of it, or the depth and distance of it, you must keep going even if you feel you're walking without direction, lost and disoriented. Of course, you can stop and take short rest stops, we all get exhausted, but stay focused on getting to the other side…take one breath at a time, one step at a time, and soon you will discover that when you least expect it a dim light will appear, making your path easier to follow.

The grief journey is long, painful and exhausting. Eight years after Sergio's death I still feel I am on that journey but I will not give up.

Athletes, such as boxers continue fighting during their boxing match despite pain and injuries; they are trained to move past the physical pain and ignore injuries to the point of a knockout. A knockout is when you know the boxer has given all he has. As mourners, we have to learn to live through the emotional pain, and keep fighting against our tendencies to give up and throw in the towel. Even when we feel like we are losing the fight, we must stay focused on our goal to survive despite our tragic loss and crippling pain. This goal is attainable but the journey is slow. We can be victors despite the punches that can painfully knock the wind right out of us and severely punish us in each round of this fight. Stand up I say; yes, stand up, get your second wind and take heart in knowing that there is an entire society of survivors rooting for you, believing that you can make it. Find the strength within yourself to reach out to God for resiliency and strength. We are not done yet; this fight is not over but it's up to you how that final round will end.

Beware that along the way you will encounter numerous detours and roadblocks and at some point you will undoubtedly feel like you've lost ground. Such obstructions may come just as we enter into a new phase in our grieving journey, and although you may feel you have started back at the beginning, remember that it's all part of the healing process that must take place in order to overcome and get to the

I give you a rose. Each petal is a layer of the grieving phases. As it withers away, so should your crippling agony.

next benchmark…this is normal. The warning sign to look for is a deep depression that sets in, or destructive behavior that begins to affect yourself and those around you. Seek medical help if you are having serious thoughts of suicide or if you have contemplated hurting others. Although it is normal to have occasional thoughts of such things, I can say that through the many years I have spent at support group meetings, listening to other parents who have lost a child through many different types of deaths, most everyone has expressed a thought of suicide at one point or another. It is also normal to feel like you would like to take revenge on someone that has hurt your child but the warning sign is when you actually contemplate and begin formulating a plan of action. Immediately seek help either for yourself or someone you may be concerned about if this happens. Life is fragile and the mind can be more fragile when overwhelmed with grief in addition to life's many challenges.

Don't take anything for granted and take very good care of yourself, particularly during the first few months. Try to eat well, get plenty of sleep, and exercise even if that simply means going for long walks. This will all help your immune and nervous system to stay healthy. Exhaustion and depression can set in rather quickly if you don't take precautions and heed the warning signs. If you don't have someone in which to confide your innermost thoughts, I would suggest that you journal your thoughts. It is harder for some to be able to express their feelings but we all know there are different forms of expression. Some can verbally convey a message and talk to others openly; while others find it easier put their thoughts into writing. Any of the options mentioned will help release some of the tension and anxiety during the critical first year.

Keeping the lines of communication open is important for the bereaved as well as for family and friends. When my husband and I made the decision to move out of state and were settled in our new community, I remember having a phone conversation with Sara, one of my sisters-in-law, and I remember saying that I felt as if her mom, my husband's mother, was resentful towards me. She shared that they were hurt emotionally when we made the decision to move away. I was surprised by that comment because we presumed that everyone knew what we were going through and thought that they understood. I suppose better communication could have avoided this; but by not explaining the reasons we had for moving, they formed their own opinions. She and I have always been close friends and the last thing I wanted was for them to feel anything but our love and respect. I explained that the reason we left was due to concern over the kids' safety and that we felt we needed to put distance between the killer and our immediate family. I shared that I had run into those people at the mall one time and that I felt panic at the thought of them coming near my kids; that I hated the fact that I feared every time my children left my side and that I needed some peace through that stressful situation. Once I explained it she was relieved but said she wished we would have told them at the time. I agreed.

I visited Sara recently and she shared with me a time when she had spoken to Sergio some time before he died; she said she told him that she was there for him in case he ever needed to talk. She said he held her hands and reciprocated the gesture. She told me that she felt this strong young man offer her support. I was blessed to hear that she saw him as I did, a strong and kind young man.

As bereaved individuals, we cannot expect others to read our mind and tip-toe around this unfamiliar terrain we are traveling through. Be appreciative of those willing to assist you and help make

things easier by communicating your needs and wants. It is very difficult for someone who is sincerely trying to help but does not know
the best way to do so. The last thing they want is to add any unnecessary stress into our already delicate state of mind. There are many
ways that others can help if you would allow them to. These can be
simple things that anyone can do and could cross off some of the
items from your To-Do list.

Once you are well enough to get out the door, get out and help
others. No matter how big or small the level of commitment, there is
great need and all help is useful and greatly appreciated. You can also
think about doing something to memorialize a loved one. Build a
memorial garden either for your loved one or for others. You can join
a balloon release offered in the community by support groups or you
can organize your own. A fundraiser and donation to a non-profit
organization in memory of your loved one provides much needed
help to the local community and may serve your purpose well.

It is God's desire that you chose a trajectory filled with purpose
and meaning. What we do now is the stark difference between the victims and the perpetrators. I have heard that the worth of a man's life
is set by his own perspective but I would interject that it would be
much more valuable if seen through God's perspective; for only He
knows our full potential and our capacity to fulfill it because He made
us with a purpose—each one of us stamped with our very own story,
His manuscript to a number one seller—a book—a masterpiece!
What is your book about? Does it read well? Does it project a cohesive message? What is written in those chapters yet to be completed?
God gave us free will so that we may choose our actions. But remember to choose wisely so your final chapters are meaningful, thereby
adding value to your testimony and the closing statement. Are you

confident that your book will earn great reviews?

Make your choice count; you can build a legacy that is truly representative of your loved one's character. It will speak volumes of the type of person he or she was and will pay tribute to them forever.

Have you ever been unable to move forward on a project because of fear? Whatever the fear is, it can take hold of you and can control the decisions you make, ultimately controlling your life.

For over two years I had been afraid to move forward with writing this book for fear that the people that were responsible for my son's death would find out and would want to bring harm to me and my family. I prayed about this project and talked to my daughter about my concerns and the potential consequences; she never hesitated as she encouraged me to write the book. After a year I finally made the decision to move forward and to trust in the Lord. A week after I made the decision to take that leap of faith—despite my fears—I attended our Sunday service at the church where I had received confirmation of the decision I had made. The subject that the pastor preached on that morning was in reference to releasing your greatest fears!

What is your fear? What is holding you back from fulfilling your purpose? Don't let the enemy rob you of the potential blessings that can come from serving God. Although the work may not always be easy and the path may not always be clear, you can finish this race knowing that you gave it your best and that you did not let your circumstances define you, but rather, you took decisive action to define your path with guidance and wisdom from God.

The killer intended to end my son's life, and he succeeded at that. However, I believe that life after death may be more powerful still. The killer did not count on our resolve; he didn't know who we are and most importantly, he knew little about God's power. The killer

and his conspirators underestimated the purpose that I would eventually come to undertake. I have earned the spirit, courage and fortitude God has equipped me with in order to serve others in their time of need. Love is the strongest, most resilient bond that ties us to our loved ones; neither time, nor distance, nor death can break that connection. More than just a bond, love is a gift and one that God prefers above all other gifts, so it's no surprise that we hurt so much when we lose a loved one. I believe we were created with a capacity to love in such a profound and genuine way that it's intricately imbedded in our essence.

My son's death brought us to an unfathomable place where we were faced with having to make life-changing, soul-searching, and pivotal decisions that would determine the rest of our lives and each with potentially serious consequences for our family unit. We were determined not to take the easy way out and worked hard toward living a productive life with a positive outcome. This in itself gives credence to the Lord we serve. Sergio's death compels us to find our true moral character and empowers us to reach beyond the measure of our own strength. Because his life mattered then so does his death. We are evolving into better human beings because his spirit brings out the best in us. Even while we live with profound sadness, we have an insatiable determination not to let his death be in vain, so we step outside our comfort zone in hopes of making a difference in someone else's life by sharing what we've learned..

I chose to direct the anger and frustration that I felt into charity work instead so that my son's memory will be well represented. Just as I mentioned at the beginning of this book; Sergio used to say that life is short—true, it is—but heaven is forever! While living our earthy lives we should make every effort not to waste it- maybe it's a test that

God has given us. I honestly feel that the best revenge is to find great ways to honor his memory; to somehow pick up where he left off and build a legacy that speaks greatly of God's love and power in our life.

Conceivably, the killer did not consider the fact that *"with God all things are possible"* (Matthew 19:26). That God can use a homicide, a murder, or even a suicide to help save souls—you can kill a body, but you cannot kill a soul! Yes, the killer may have been acquitted, but the truth remains and it speaks ever so loudly. More importantly, God knows the truth and this man will one day stand before Him to give an account for what he did; on that day he will not be able to lie, deceive or work the system as he did in the criminal court. On that appointed day he will not have his cronies with him to back him up. (2 Corinthians 5-10; KJV) *"For we must all appear before the judgment seat of Christ; that every one may receive the things done in his body, according to that he hath done, whether it be good or bad."* On that day, God will give us justice! Ultimately, the killer loses because while he is free now, in a sense, his spirit will forever be in bondage and what he meant for evil, God is using for good and it will carry on for years to come and will help fulfill God's purpose and we pray that some may come to see the glory of God, His divine purpose and the power of the cross.

The Bible reminds that us that for everything there is a season (Ecclesiastes 3:1-8, 12, 15-17; KJV).

> [1] *To everything there is a season, and a time to every purpose under the heaven:* [2] *A time to be born, and a time to die; a time to plant, and a time to pluck up that which is planted;* [3] *A time to kill, and a time to heal; a time to break down, and a time to build up;* [4] *A time to weep, and a time to laugh; a time to*

mourn, and a time to dance; *5 A time to cast away stones, and a time to gather stones together; a time to embrace, and a time to refrain from embracing;*

6 A time to get, and a time to lose; a time to keep, and a time to cast away; 7 A time to rend, and a time to sew; a time to keep silence, and a time to speak; 8 A time to love, and a time to hate; a time of war, and a time of peace.

12 I know that there is no good in them, but for a man to rejoice, and to do well in his life. 15 That which hath been is now; and that which is to be hath already been; and God requireth that which is past. 16 And moreover I saw under the sun the place of judgment, that wickedness was there; and the place of righteousness, that iniquity was there. 17 I said in mine heart, God shall judge the righteous and the wicked: for there is a time there for every purpose and for every work.

A time for everything—I ponder on the meaning of those words. Time is something we can never take back; we cannot buy it or sell it. It can help and it can hurt—but for now—I am using the time God has given me to live the rest of my life with purpose and we can never have too much time for that. My son was killed, but his spirit lives on and is dwelling in the house of the Lord. Sergio believed in God the Father, Jesus the Son, and in the

Holy Spirit. We are convinced that death is not the end, it is a passage to the beginning; *"We are confident, I say, and willing rather to be absent from the body, and to be present with the LORD,"* (2 Corinthians 5:8; KJV). We are in total dependence on the Lord for our salvation and it helps to know that we will be united with Him immediately upon our death.

Much work remains to be done here on earth while we are still living. As the countdown of my life continues in motion, I am painfully aware that life is short and fragile and that one day I too will be gone. I have a greater sense of urgency to accomplish the tasks that God has set before me. I can't help wanting to go to Heaven and be with Him and with my son again but I am torn because I have three wonderful kids here that I love just the same. I remind myself that my family here needs me a lot more than Sergio does now because he is in a perfect body and a perfect place; a place where time does not matter... and that helps me feel better. When I am called to go home, for Sergio it will be but a moment since he last saw me; but for me, a lifetime.

The following are some of the things that have helped me during my grieving journey and I thought I'd share them with you.

For the bereaved, I humbly offer the following five suggestions:

- **Be willing to accept help. You don't want to hinder someone's blessing when they kindly offer their support.** *I remember I felt bad when family and friends offered to help me after my son died. I recall my cousin saying to me, "I am being obedient to the Lord and I offer my help sincerely, let me do my work as unto the Lord." I was also told by my pastor that every time I rejected someone's help, I was interfering with the work between that person and*

the Lord.

• **Pray for strength, peace, and healing. God will help you
and will bring the right individuals into your path.** *You will know
when God sends you these individuals because they will somehow be able to relate
to your loss and will have a lot of things in common. This may be a calling or
ministry for those individuals.*

• **Most of the time, you will not be in the mood to do anything other than just survive the day; after an appropriate
amount of time, you should begin to wisely push yourself to do
some of the things you used to enjoy doing, slowly. If someone
offers to take you to dinner or a movie, give yourself the opportunity to get out and begin that journey.** *A few months after my son's
death, my cousin Nancy invited us to the movies. After a few invites I finally
accepted, more for the kids than for myself. We went to see the movie Shrek, and
I remember that it was very difficult to get out of the house and go out to a movie
when my heart was so broken inside, but half-way through the movie, I found
myself thinking what a wonderful thing she had done for us because I needed to
hear my other kids laugh again and that made me feel better.*

• **It is normal to feel awkward and even guilty when you
begin the healing journey, but you must take the small steps
that will help you to heal. This does not mean—in any way—that
you are abandoning your loved one. You would want the same
for them, right?** *The biggest hindrance for me was the feeling of guilt. I felt
bad if I even thought of doing something that would be soothing, let alone fun. I
know it's irrational, but I felt as though I was abandoning my son. I did not
believe I could ever smile, laugh, or enjoy life again. It took months, but I felt I
had to offer my other children more than the scraps of joy I was giving them by
denying them and myself any type of healthy lifestyle. I had to realize that my
other children also deserved the best I could give, even while I was grieving. It was*

not fair to them to also lose their mother after losing their brother. I had to force myself to find a healthy balance because I love them too.

• **Lean on the Lord for strength and ask God to help you find the right path.** *This was for me—and continues to be—the most important part of my survival. I would not have made it this far had it not been for my faith in God. Years later, I still struggle with my son's death and I probably always will. But I still go to the Lord for daily strength.*

I feel obliged to fulfill the purpose that God has set before me. I believe that giving back is important because when our time of need has come and gone and we have gained the critical tools necessary from those that went before us; it is beautiful to see that when we begin to gain some strength during our journey, we can step outside of our own grief to comfort others and add to the links in the chain of survivors.

Closing Thought
"The pain is real and the sorrow runs deep,
but even when you don't want to live,
God can give you peace and heal the pain in your heart.
You can choose to be a survivor."

Chapter Eighteen

HOW CAN YOU HELP?

Whether you or someone you know has lost a loved one, you can make a difference in the life of a bereaved person. One of the biggest misconceptions is that people don't want to mention our loved one's name for fear that it will sadden us. News Flash!—we are already sad but it warms the heart to hear our loved one's name and to know that they have not been forgotten. Sometimes just being there to listen can make all the difference in the world.

Encourage them to attend a support group and go with them. At times, the best therapy is walking into a room full of people that are going through similar circumstances and who understand exactly what a bereaved person feels because they are on the same path. It's important for bereaved individuals to know that they are not alone in this difficult journey. All you have to do is reach out and be willing to walk along that road with them. It's up to you to make it happen.

For those willing to help:

• Offer to **help coordinate the funeral arrangements,** even on a small scale. *This can be the most daunting task to undertake for the newly bereaved, especially if the death was sudden and unexpected. The smallest task can help alleviate an already overwhelming burden on the immediate family and your help can make a big difference.*

• **Visit** often and be willing to **listen actively and attentively** to the person in mourning. *During the initial few days after the death, we are* *surrounded by family and friends, and more often than not, once the funeral is over and everyone leaves, that is when the hardest part of the journey begins because now we are left to face the rest of our life on our own.*

• If you are able to, offer to help with **babysitting, dog sitting, chores, or perhaps even financially**. *These items may seem insignificant in the grand scheme of things, but for a person in mourning, this may be the help the bereaved person needs in order to get a handle on the responsibilities that mount on top of the overwhelming grief.*

• Remember to **mention their loved one BY NAME**. *Contrary to popular belief, most people that have lost a loved one do not want to stop hearing their loved one's name, despite the sadness. It warms the heart to know that their loved one is still remembered by others.*

• Offer to **accompany them when they visit their loved one's grave**. *This may or may not be easily granted, depending on the level of trust and closeness you share with the bereaved individual because this is a very intimate and private area of one's grief; tread carefully, but if handled tactfully, you may see a welcomed response.*

• Offer to **help if and when the bereaved is ready and willing to pack away their loved one's belongings**. *But know that this will be an excruciatingly painful task for the bereaved, and it will take a lot of love, patience, and understanding to get through that experience. It is very important for someone to be there with that person so they are not left to deal with such devastation alone.*

• Research literature relevant to the type of death suffered so you can **become familiar with the HUG (Human Understanding of Grief**—Not an official term, just an acronym I created) **factor**. *Both you and the bereaved will benefit greatly from such resources. There is great material published in all areas of death. A few weeks after the funeral I was able to open a book that a friend gave me, it made me feel better knowing that others were* *able to survive a similar loss, it also helped me realize that I wasn't going crazy feeling so overwhelmed with grief.*

• Offer your **unconditional love and pray for them and with them.** *There is power in prayer and one can never get too much of it. If you feel you are hitting a wall every time you offer your help and it gets rejected, perhaps the best thing you can do is pray for that person and that family. God will work in their broken hearts. Don't give up on them.*

• Offer to help during **holidays, anniversaries, birthdays, and other special occasions.** *Ask what it is that they would need your help with. This is particularly true during the first year.*

• Because God created each of us differently, it is natural that we—including children—would also grieve differently. **Be patient.** *Death is devastating for us all. For the person and family experiencing the death of a loved one, there is no such thing as closure and they may never get over it. They will, however, need to learn to live with it and will need to create a new way of life that will help them move on. Please don't ever tell a person that they should "be over it by now." These are very hurtful and insensitive words and the person may end up resenting you for saying such a thing. Instead, let them know they are doing well and remind them that they have come a long way; they need your support and encouragement, not your criticism. Although I understand there are some people that turn to a destructive path and very counterproductive ways of mourning, these are the instances where counseling would be most helpful.*

For Grief Support Providers:

We know that death is as part of life as life itself and while the birth of a child can be a joyous occasion and tends to change our perspective in life; the death of a child brings an even greater impact. The emotions wrapped in the death of a child are devastating, impactful, and life-altering. At the birth of a child, you are normally given nine

months to prepare all the necessary elements to welcome the child into this world and into your life. However, the death of a child is something that no parent can ever prepare for and you never get used to the idea of him or her leaving this world before you, their parent. The strong emotions experienced by the birth of your child are deep and meaningful and you can spend the rest of your life enjoying your child; the death of a child is that much more intense, especially at an unexpected or sudden death of your precious son or daughter but in this case, you can also spend life in deep sadness caused by the emptiness that is left behind.

As I said before, death is such a difficult subject to discuss and most people don't know how to address the situation when death hits home or the home of a loved one. For bereaved individuals surviving such a loss requires the support of family, friends, and the entire community. As I've said previously, because we are all different it is important to understand that we also grieve differently. Some individuals will need to seek help from external resources in order to survive and rebuild their shattered lives. Getting to that place however, will require a lengthy process that encompasses different phases through the mourning and healing process and often, a mourner can go back and forth to certain phases throughout their life.

As a survivor profoundly and passionately committed to this cause and I endeavor to be a voice for those most affected and most vulnerable; being a voice to the victims that have been slain is important but standing with the survivors that need our help is crucial. If we are to build on the hard work of many that have undertaken the difficult task of aiding the grieving community we must, with the best of intentions, be willing to use our tragic stories and grief experiences for posterity measures. We must be willing to go through the pain every time we tell our story. This may seem like a daunting task, but knowing that it can help others survive their grief can help alleviate the apprehension that can sometimes prevent someone from taking action.

For some individuals it is extremely difficult to reach out for help because of pride, shame, lack of financial resources, or for many other reasons. Some of us have tried to obtain grief counseling from various resources in the professional community, but for a large number of individuals, the experience has been less than favorable, at best. I speak from personal experience and for the hundreds of bereaved individuals that I have met who have candidly shared their concern and disappointment in this area of their grieving process. In fact, in some cases the outcome of such encounters have been counter-productive and detrimental to the mourner's healing progress. I speak of counseling sessions that some bereaved individuals have had with grieving counselors, psychologists, psychiatrists, licensed clinical social workers, primary care physicians, community leaders, as well as others that may have plenty of textbook knowledge but not personal experience on the death of a child. I also speak of those that are ill-equipped to render advice with genuine compassion and understanding.

I can go on and on about some of the horror stories I have heard from the countless number of individuals to which I have spoken. But suffice it to say that some professionals assume such roles with pride and arrogance characterized by some as the "know it all" syndrome when in fact that professional may never have experienced the death of a loved one, let alone, the death of a child; leaving the griever confused and frustrated and at times causing more harm than good. In fact, pastors, priests, and other religious leaders may also fall under

this concern when these leaders don't know how to handle such a topic. They sometimes find it easier to cast judgment on the bereaved by questioning their faith, as was in my case and that of many others I know. Now, I am not saying that all professionals mentioned above fall into this category, not by any means, but for those that do, I offer a sincere suggestion of the perspective mentioned in this section as it may be of value, particularly for those that will reach out to you for help.

Keep in mind that people mourning the death of a child, particularly at the beginning stages, are already in a fragile, confused, and debilitated state of mind and that is the reason we may reach out for assistance in the first place. We may feel the need for guidance and direction in rebuilding our capacity to navigate the rest of our lives.

It is my hope that this book and this section may open up opportunities for dialogue and a new perspective from the traditional methods in practice and of "cross-the-board judgment" of bereaved individuals that are too often labeled as "mental," "unstable," or in the case of religion, "lacking faith," when in fact that may not be the case at all; they may be merely going through the normal grieving process that most of us have to go through in order to make it to the other side. I am well aware that some individuals will require medication, and rightfully so but at times some physicians are too quick to pull out the prescription pad before the patient is even done talking, as was in my case. I suppose that for some doctors it may be easier or faster to medicate or pacify the patient rather than take the time to listen all the way through to the end of their sentence. I have found that opposing this sacred system is frowned upon but I offer my perspective; take it for what it's worth.

I never imagined I would be speaking on or writing about this subject, but here I am, a bereaved mother whose son was viciously killed and I have suffered mercilessly through this process. My family and I became a part of the rising number in the statistics of gang and domestic violence; unwilling participants through no fault of our own left to figure out how to live through the devastation and chaos that the violent death of a loved has left for us. I have learned harsh lessons along the way yet I have gained courage from the love that my family gives me to take on this cause and valiantly speak out for all those traveling this journey. I walk on the heels of other courageous men and women who have paved the way for the grieving community in solidarity and with a sincere desire to help those offering grief support services which in turn will help us. I, along with many others, am trying to reach people during the most turbulent and distressing time of their lives through the experiences of those of us that are further along the path.

I call out to those in the capacity to help us and that are willing to consider other perspectives; together we can transform the status-quo so that alternative therapeutic and rehabilitation methods can emerge from a collaborative effort of all those interested and those most affected.

For a mourner, a grieving war rages inside us that forces us to make life-changing decisions that we may or may not be capable of making depending on the intensity of our grief, our pain tolerance, or the strength of our resolve. We would not reach out for help if we did not feel it absolutely necessary. We are not arbitrarily deciding to dump our responsibilities or issues onto a counselor, therapist, or religious leader. On the contrary, I believe I speak for a lot of people when I say that it takes a responsible person to admit they need help through the grief and that they are searching for productive ways to

cope with such a loss. I know there are some people that abuse certain situations, even as mourners. I have seen that end of the spectrum as well. I have met some moms that even years after the death of their child, are in such an incapacitated state and not really functional; leaving the responsibility on others to undertake but at times, unfortunately, these are their surviving children. This extreme I find unacceptable because we, as parents are to take on the responsibility and the bulk of the load, whether we want to or not; it is not fair to our surviving children to expect them to take care of us on top of their own grief and loss. We have no right to dump this burden on them. I have always found it distasteful when a bereaved person uses their grief as a crutch or a reason to abuse a situation or the people around them.

Moving past that, I believe that together patients and grief support providers can find concrete ways to a healthy healing process. Give us the necessary tools, provide us with sincere compassion and understanding but don't enable us or make us dependent upon medication and other habit forming substances when they are unnecessary because sometimes that recourse may make matters worse, not just for the individual but those around him or her.

Talk to us, listen to us, be willing to feel our pain, and learn from us so that your efforts yield better results for the long haul. Earn the trust that we are willing to give, but don't patronize us with arrogant and detached behaviors that hide behind layers of excuses in efforts to create shortcuts to these critical issues. Don't talk down to us and make us feel like we don't know what we're talking about; we do, and we want to share it with you so that you gain deeper understanding of this phenomenon called death and the devastating grief it leaves for survivors. If we are able to begin change in this field and make significant progress in the healing process, we must begin to change the taboo that still exists and that hinders many people from reaching out for help, much needed help. We must create a trusting and healthy environment for bereaved individuals and make them feel like this is a safe haven rather than a place where they go for judgment, condemnation, and co-dependency. We may be able to build on the platform of candidness without the fear of severe repercussions, and I say this cautiously because I don't presume to know the emotional state of mind of any patient; that I will respectfully leave that for the professionals to decide.

However, I have heard time and again that many bereaved individuals are afraid to seek the much needed help because they fear if they say something wrong, they may face consequences they are not willing to risk. Case in point is the story of Michaela, whose story we will share in detail in the next book, *Tiers of Violence*. Tragically, she witnessed the murders of her husband and her 17 year-old daughter. She counseled in the beginning stages of her grief, when it was most intense and she was labeled as "unstable." She talked about going through mandatory court proceedings with mandatory psychiatric sessions to prove that she was fit to resume her role as a mother to her surviving 9 year-old son but it took months for her to get her son back. The damage that was done to her is incomprehensible. The damage it did to the grief community is even bigger because everyone that heard her story was left feeling insecure about "the system," and many would not dare step foot into a counseling session. But this is just one example in this problem area. I concede that said professionals must be cautious for liability reasons, and I want to make it clear that I am not talking about the legitimate instances where a patient's condition warrants such drastic measures by their doctors and thera-

pists. I am not saying that we have to ignore warning signs that can pose a risk but I am suggesting that providers merely consider alternate solutions and perspectives for those that don't really fall under that severe category.

For this reason, the non-profit grief support groups that graciously offer their services have such favorable ratings; it's because we are allowed to openly and safely discuss our feelings without fear of retribution. Perhaps there is a lesson to be learned here. This is a real crisis and real solutions must be found if we are to make a real difference. I invite all grief support providers to join some of these support group meetings on a regular basis and learn from the candid dialogue shared by your target demographics. I believe that textbook knowledge alone will never teach you everything you need to learn about this subject until you spend time with real mourners, and these meetings are a great place to start.

In the old days, people handled death crimes differently; if a person was murdered the surviving family would avenge their loved ones, that was their right. But being the civilized country that we are, we must find new ways to handle such death tragedies. So how do we do that? Even back in the old days, people obviously had such strong thoughts and feelings; they were not asked to suppress them or face consequences for mentioning such thoughts. How then, do we reconcile our human nature with that of a judgmental society? Believe me when I say that as bereaved individuals, it is a miserable and frustrating place we find ourselves in, but we continue to search for healthy solutions because we don't want to be part of the problem.

We ask that you are not fooled into thinking that you know better or that it is easier to turn a blind eye to a new perspective for fear that it may not be worth your time. You may be a respected professional in your field and you may have received numerous accolades to prove it; but unless you have experienced the loss of a child yourself, you may not know better. You may have been able to gain enough knowledge to provide wise counsel to your patients, great as it may be, there is still a missing element, a level of understanding that you have not acquired because you have not suffered it yourself. But you can gain enough of it to provide better counsel if you go deep enough to get to the root of the grief. If you are willing to get to that level in your profession and become better equipped to provide "the best" you can give, you must be willing to go through the fire with your patients and you must be willing to submerge yourself in their pain so that you may gain in-depth knowledge and a profound understanding of what that grief is all about. If you are willing to take that journey with us then we are willing to share our pain and our experiences with you.

What I am proposing is building upon existing measures that successfully meet the needs of the bereaved; and establishing pillars of strength that provide healing with dignity, empathy, and an authentic desire to help the person in need rather than for personal gain. I call upon the professionals in the field and those seeking to enter this field to fight this noble cause and to advocate on our behalf. Tobe an integral part of our journey, to construct a new doctrine that is transformational and inspirational; one that can earn the trust and respect of the grieving community. I challenge you to take this platform to new heights and aim to impact survivors in a more healthy and meaningful way.

Is this difficult? It certainly can be, but only as difficult as you perceive it to be. However, positive and significant advancements can be made in this field and it is within your reach to be part of the innovators able and willing to take on the cause for the common good. By

strongly supporting our efforts for survival you can be the professional, which helps us in our healing journey or that which can continue to hinder that process. The choice is yours but remember that our form of existence or quality of life may depend on it.

Closing Thought and a Call-To-Action
"I speak for the victims that have been slain; I stand with the survivors that need our help. Stand with me now and let the victims know you care."

EPILOGUE

At times it seems as though it's been an eternity since my son's death. It has been a long and agonizing journey. I miss him at every special occasion, and I am coming to terms with the fact that the more time goes by, the more I miss him. Other times it can feel like it was just yesterday and the pain emerges all over again, then I begin the process of redirecting my focus and reminding myself to keep going, to be strong and hold steadfast. I think of this internal struggle as the human factor, the battle between a mother's need and the spiritual wisdom of setting my sight on heaven.

Here and now: Moving forward and making a difference are what I am focused on now. Just as the glimpse of what I saw when I delivered the eulogy at my son's funeral and the purpose I've determined, I am now speaking out and staying busy. I take comfort knowing that every time I put effort into a project, it helps sand down the rough edges of my cross, making it more bearable. My broken heart mends by keeping Sergio's memory alive and giving testimony to his life; it exemplifies the character behind the man.

I speak at conferences and churches sharing the devastation caused by domestic and gang violence which shatters lives and alters one's existence, but more importantly, I speak about the power of God's love.

I am encouraged to hear some of the comments after each speaking engagement and it helps keep me going. Giving a presentation about my son's homicide is extremely difficult and always painful. But I feel it's important to share the story in hopes that it may help others experiencing the loss of a loved one and possibly give them hope that they too can survive. I also hope that it may help prevent domestic or gang violence by sharing with the community some of the warning signs that may be prevalent in someone's life. More than a "don't let this happen to you" message, it's a message that it can happen to anyone, even when you think you're taking all the necessary measures to lead a safe life.

I have not seen my sister Lisa since the day of the trial; I know not what occupies her time or what she has done with her life. I do however, wonder how her children are doing and how these atrocities have affected their lives. I know they were not to blame and I hate that they have been subjected to such a dismal environment. I can't even imagine what they have had to endure growing up in the reality and ugliness of that world, with questionable role models making life-altering decisions that may impact their lives negatively.

Has she realized how many lives she has affected and perhaps even damaged, or does she even care? Does she care about her children's future? I wonder if she ever asked her oldest son how Sergio's death affected him since he too was very close to Sergio. I heard rumors that her son had talked about suicide at one point and I reached out to him directly. I could not bear the thought of having his life destroyed as well. Yes, her son was affected; I am sure of it; I just pray that they are able to escape that cycle sooner rather than later so they can have a fighting chance at a somewhat normal life.

I also do not know if the killer has ever regretted his actions or if he thinks about taking Sergio's life. I wonder if he ever suffers from nightmares the way that we have or if he ever wished to die as I have.

Has he ever looked at his hands and thought back to the moment he took Sergio's life—with those same hands—and feel repugnance? I wonder what it must have been like for him the first time he saw himself in the mirror after becoming a killer...I really wonder.

As far as the others involved in the homicide, I heard that some of them still find themselves on a destructive path, which brings validity to the well-founded concerns that my husband and I had for the safety of our other children.

Arguably, moving out of the state after the killer was arrested, I suppose can be interpreted in different ways, depending on one's life experiences; some believe that we were foolish to let the perpetrators run us out of our own home; while others expressed their support for our decisions. All I can say is that you would have to live through that situation yourself in order to fully grasp the level of concern—and even panic—that can set into a parent's heart when their children are in danger.

For me personally, the distance also brought some peace knowing that we would never run into them. There is nothing more important to my husband and I than the safety of our children. Besides, they had already killed one of our children so there was no doubt in our mind that they would do it again, given the opportunity. Hearing the news of their destructive lives so many years later really saddens me; it is horrific to imagine how far they intend to let the lives of many, as well as their own be hurt or destroyed.

So I am left with a quandary- what to do with the thoughts that occasionally cross my mind about them? Do I loathe them, or do I pray for them? Pray for them, really? I could easily say, "Go to hell, and let them be imprisoned by their own evil," but that does not bring my son back, it does not take the pain away and it does not erase the damage done. It will not eliminate the devastation they may continue to cause in the interim—while we wait for Heaven. However, if God would work in their hearts and bring them to repentance, only then could they be convicted of their vile acts of violence and feel the weight of their actions. Then their spirits would grieve all the damage they have caused others and they would ultimately pay for what they have done. I do pray that they come to a place of conviction, and bring about a change in their lives. Only then could we rest knowing that we are no longer in danger and only then can they begin their own healing and restoration. I believe God has the power to do that, and I believe that there is power in prayer. I want to believe that they have the ability to change and to love. I really do.

Years later we are doing better. We are busy with family life, church, and taking those leaps of faith that each time takes us to another level of healing. There is a lot of work to be done in this field; we all have something to offer and now is the perfect time to make a difference in someone's life. I have never regretted those times when I've stepped out in faith to help others even when it was inconvenient or inconceivable that I could offer something while I felt so broken. On the other hand, I have regretted those times when I found myself recognizing missed opportunities to serve others. That's not to say that we have to say "yes" to everything, but it does mean that we should be willing to help no matter how insignificant our contributions may seem or at what phase in our grieving we may find ourselves.

I am currently doing advocacy work for gang and domestic violence prevention. I speak at conferences, retreats, churches, and support groups across the nation in an effort to bring hope for survival and inspiration for revival.

IN CLOSING

As I reached the end of my research for this book, I took my last trip across the country to conduct my last two interviews. I sat at a busy airport waiting for my plane to board and I made full use of the time by drafting the interview questions so that I would be fully prepared when I met my interviewees.

As I prepared to type however, I began to miss my family. I would be far away from them for days and I worried, should an emergency arise. I thought to myself that I had better make that trip count; that I should make sure that the time I spent away from them was purposeful and productive.

I was determined to finish this book and to polish off the pages I carefully drafted over the past two years. Chisel them like a finely sculpted diamond; each cut revealing a different angle, reflecting a different light. Polish them to a brilliant revelation of my soul; a reflection of my spirit, which was distraught and inconsolable at Sergio's death; yet by his loving spirit I was encouraged to embark upon a healing journey that has brought me to a bright, marvelous illumination of God's truth.

I took my torment to the Lord and He gave me peace; I trusted Him with the Tiers of Sorrow that were forced upon me, and He trusted me to do His work.

"Think of me, my sweet, as I of you,
and know that even in my dreams, I long for you."

In Loving Memory of Sergio Jr.

ABOUT THE AUTHOR

Sandra Toscano was born in Jalisco, Mexico. She enjoys spending time with her husband of thirty one years, her three surviving children, and two grandchildren. Volunteering as a victims' advocate, Sandra endeavors to bring awareness about the aftermath of violence and the death of a child. She promotes the significant work of various grief support groups that offer a wide array of services to meet the needs of the bereaved. She believes it's important to be proactive and work to gain ground in the areas of gang and domestic violence prevention.

Sandra is passionate about sharing her story and sending a message of faith, hope, love, and survival. In doing so, she believes her son's death is not in vain.

Recipient of the "Top 50 Most Influential Women" for 2011.

CONTRIBUTORS

ARNO ARR MICHAELS IV

"Tenderness and kindness are not signs of weakness and despair, but manifestations of strength and resolutions."
—Khalil Gibran (1883-1931)

My relationship with violence is entering its 43rd year. Though I grew up in a privileged environment, the emotional violence of alcoholism drove me away from loving parents and towards an irresponsible practice of hate and self-destruction. I went from being a bully on the school bus in kindergarten, to getting in schoolyard fights, to vandalism and burglary, to assuming the identity of a violent racist skinhead at age 16. Until my mid-twenties, I founded and led hate groups and bellowed white supremacist rage as front-man for a hate-metal band that had sold over 20,000 records worldwide by the mid-nineties.

Single parenthood, love for my daughter, and the forgiveness shown by people I once hated all helped to turn my life around, bringing me to embrace diversity and practice gratitude for all life. I renounced racism in 1995. Today I am a speaker, author of My Life After Hate, and practitioner of character development, which hones the strength, courage, and honor necessary to practice peace. I am very fortunate to be able to travel and share my story in an effort to be an asset to the world around me. I travel across the country as I participate in gang prevention conferences, among others, and it was at one of these conferences where I met Sandra Toscano.

As I share my story of transformation, Sandra shared her story of anguish, telling of the nightmarish circumstances of her son's homicide by a confessed gang member, and the rampant injustice that followed as the killer gamed the system and continued to threaten her and her family during his fugitive period. Fortunately, for Sandra and for everyone who has the honor of meeting her, this heartbroken mother was able to engage with human spirituality and find the strength to not only carry on after losing her son, but also to become a beacon to guide others suffering such catastrophic loss to a place of love and healing. As Sandra so beautifully demonstrates, even the most devastating agony can be transformed to an inspiration, powerful enough to change perpetrators into peacemakers and victims into survivors.

Having led the life of a heartless criminal capable of complete disregard for the suffering of my fellow human beings, Sandra's story challenges me to reconcile my past. I could have been the miserable disconnected being responsible for a mother's grief, had it not been for the grace of compassion and forgiveness. Instead I have come to work alongside Sandra, helping to divert others from violence. The open honesty *Tiers of Sorrow* delivers has the power to lead others engaged in hostility to a more peaceful place, just as I have been led.

For the past four years, my relationship with violence has evolved to one of loving opposition. Thanks to examples of courage like the one set by Sandra, today I understand that violence is a cyclical process, and that the most effective way to disrupt this process is to answer aggression with compassion.

—ARNO ARR MICHAELS IV/ Speaker, Author, and Peace Advocate/ arno@mylifeafterhate.com/ Web: mylifeafterhate.com/ Facebook: www.facebook.com/ mylifeafterhate/ Twitter: @mylifeafterhate/ YouTube: mylifeafterhate

MARK BRIDGEMAN

Championing a cause to aid families, communities, law enforcement, and fight against gang and domestic violence.

As a twenty-five year veteran police officer, I have seen many instances when parents do all the right things yet their children fall victim to the senseless violence of gangs. Gang violence in the United States has, unfortunately become commonplace in many communities large and small throughout our country. When gang violence strikes, it is devastating to the families involved.

The Huerta family is the epitome of a modern American family in any town USA. The Huerta's instilled traditional family values into their children, which is a challenge in today's world. We are not perfect, and our children will challenge us as parents.

The murder or homicide of anyone is a tragedy; parents never imagine the death of their children, let alone through a violent act. Sergio Jr. was struck down at too early an age by a felon. The stress of a violent crime can rip a family apart. I have had the opportunity to speak with many survivors of gang violence, and some have lost everything. The survivors of senseless gang violence have a common denominator that carries them through- it's faith in God.

For those of faith, we never know what God will put before us; the death of a child is severe and painful, a true test of faith.

Sandra's faith was shaken and tested beyond comprehension, yet she refuses to allow the death of her son Sergio to be in vain. Sandra has championed a cause to aid families, communities, law enforcement and countless others by sharing her firsthand experiences of gang and domestic violence, however painful. Sandra does this in the name of the Lord and in memory of her son Sergio.

I invite you to get involved and help make a difference in your local community because we are all in this together.

—*MARK BRIDGEMAN/25 year veteran of the Fayetteville Police Department (NC)/President of North Carolina Gang Investigator's Association/Gang Free NC/Chair of NC Governor's Gang Task Force/Treasurer of National Alliance of Gang Investigators Association*

AGNES J. GIBBONEY

Reading the book "Tiers of Sorrow" awakened many painful memories, not only for my loss but for Sandra's as well.

I did not have the privilege of knowing Sergio prior to his death but he became very close to my heart afterwards, as if I had known him forever. Sandra and I had many similarities in our boys' deaths and I believe it brought us together with the kind of connection and bond only mothers with great grief share. Ronald was murdered in El Monte, Sergio was killed there as well; Ronald's life was cut short in April, so was Sergio's; different persons from the same gang killed our boys. We also had the same prosecutor.

Sandra and I could talk about our rawest of feelings openly, truly understanding and validating each other's feelings. When Sandra and her family moved away, I promised to take care of Sergio's gravesite. Almost 3 years ago she called asking for a "favor," to sign and be present at the cemetery for Sergio's disinterment. This was by far, the most difficult thing I have ever done, but I did it, for her and for Sergio. I felt as if I had lost a child all over again. On the other hand, I was so happy for her and her family, because Sergio was going home to be close to them. I felt such emptiness, pain and a feeling of loss. I even called the airline to see how much a round trip ticket would cost so I could be on the plane with Sergio to accompany him home, but it was too expensive. I lit a candle at home for Sergio to have a safe trip home.

To this date I miss visiting his grave, I always look up the hill and think about him, sending my love. I still have his picture in my china cabinet. Sergio is and always will be a part of my family. Sandra and I will always be mothers who had our hearts ripped apart by the tragedy that brought us together. We never gave up speaking about our boys and keeping their memories alive. Most of all, we are there for each other and the families that are touched by these tragedies called homicide and murder.

I think this book would help those grieving by following in the steps of those paving the way to a healthy healing journey by not giving up, by doing something positive with the grief, staying faithful, and reaching out to other victims' families, but most of all reaffirming that what the families are feeling, all the confusion, despair, pain, anger, hatred, or whatever else, are all normal to the grieving process.

Support groups could use *Tiers of Sorrow* as a guide, as a resource, as a topic of discussion for meetings to help families open up and to sort out their jumbled feelings. After all, our deceased loved ones did not come with instructions on how to navigate through this diffi-

cult road called grief.
—*AGNES J. GIBBONEY/Chapter Leader of Inland Empire (POMC)*

ACKNOWLEDGEMENTS

Recognition is given to the individuals that helped make this book possible. I thank each and every one of them and I would like to honor them by forever commemorating them in this book. To my immediate family for their unconditional supported and their patience as I spent endless hours at the computer and for the missed family functions during this process: to my son Andy and his wife Rosemary for their love and encouragement; to my daughter Jennie, who encouraged me to write the book and also provided amazing photography for the book. I also thank her husband Noah for the support he gave her while she spent numerous hours on concept and photography; to my son Austin for his impressive graphic design and illustration contributions, which have earned great reviews. A special thanks to my sister Veronica for her permission to use the 911 call. Additionally, I recognize my extended families: the Villaseñor and Toscano families for all their love, support, and helping to promote *Tiers of Sorrow*. And to Sergio's friends Jesse; Justin; and Chris for the years of loyalty, of love, and companionship they shared with Sergio.

To the law enforcement professionals Detective S. Page; Homicide Detective G. McFadden; Homicide Detective Barry Telis, LAPD; and Detective M. Bridgeman; they each selflessly spent several hours with me on interviews, sharing their subject matter expertise in efforts to provide a holistic perspective.

To the interviewees that shared their heartbreaking stories while reliving their own tragedies: Raul, Dolores, Yasareth, and Edith Villaseñor; to Michaela E.; and to Lu Prudhomme.

To the grief support and victim advocates that provided guidance, counsel, and contributed their testimonials and endorsements: Agnes Gibboney, for also loving and caring for my son Sergio, long after his death; to Arno Michaels who risks his own life by working against hate and violent extremists; and to Sammy Rangel, whose contribution to the Foreword page in this book helped set the tone and prepared the reader for a heart-wrenching and compelling story.

I thank Benny Hester for contributing his song lyrics used in this book and at my son's funeral; to S. Babisha for scripture and Biblical guidance. Thank you to the legal counsel that generously offered their time to review the manuscript: Jonathan E. Buchan, and Jeffrey Parsons, Attorneys at Law.

I would also like to acknowledge the writing and film professionals who graciously offered a review of this book as well as advice: Margaret Montreuil; Ann Bruce; to my good friend Sandie Adams for working long hours in proofing, while battling health problems; Brandi Rabon; Michelle Alanis; Matt Francis; and last but not least, I would like to express my gratitude to Wayne Coster Cooper., who was more than a contributor, he was a mentor and a book coach. His contributions and encouragement made the publication of this book possible.

COMING SOON

This project is planned to be a series of books that will focus on specific fields of ministry; such as:

* *Tiers of Violence* will be geared towards law enforcement; focused on the reality of life after violence as opposed to Hollywood's glamorized versions. I will include homicide, murder, suicide, and murder-suicide cases. This book will be used in training, providing a victim's perspective to Homicide Detectives, Domestic Violence Counselors, Judicial and Legislative Officials, as well as Gang Prevention educators. I have done several interviews with families of murdered victims, with convicted murderers, homicide detectives, fugitive task force officers, which will give profound insight and poignant details to help curtail gang and domestic violence.

* *Tiers of Joy* will focus on the ministry that has evolved as a result of this and many other tragic stories that have become collaborative efforts for a productive cause. It will speak of turning misery into a ministry, helping survivors and/or families grieving the death of a loved one find hope for survival and inspiration for revival. It will exemplify the joy that can come back into the lives of the bereaved when great purpose if found beyond such tragedies.

*All books will be made available in Spanish as well.

*Audio, eBook, Kindle, and Hard Cover will be made available soon.

For information about a speaking engagement for your next conference (either in English or Spanish), or for book orders please visit:

www.SandraToscanoBooks.com.
www.Instagram.com/SandraToscanoBooks
www.Facebook.com/SandraToscanoBooks

RESOURCES

Below is a starter-list that you can use as a reference. Your local community may offer other valuable resources that cater to each specific type of loss. I would highly recommend joining a local group because you can build friendships with people that you may want to spend time with.

- Parents of Murdered Children: National-natlpomc@pomc.org, (888) 818-7662
- The Compassionate Friends: National- 900 Jorie Blvd. Suite 78, Oak Brook, IL 60523 (877) 969-0010
- National Suicide Prevention Lifeline: (800) 273-8255
- Suicide.org: (800)-Suicide (800) 784-2433
- Thehotline.org for domestic violence: 1-800-799-SAFE (7233) or TTY 1-800-787-3224
- National Alliance of Gang Investigators' Association (NAGIA): Elkhorn, NE- (402) 510-8581
- California Gang Investigators' Association (CGIA): (888) 229-2442 (CGIA)
- Tennessee Gang Investigators' Association: 5251-C Hwy 153, Suite 139, Hixson,TN 37343
- Florida Gang Investigators' Association: 2220 County Road, 210 West Suite 108 PMB 329, St Johns, Florida 32259-863-272-8676
- Churches in your local community may also offer free resources that can help during the grieving process

There is a vast array of publications available, specific to each type of loss. Reach out to any of the agencies listed for more information.

CITED SOURCES

The Bible verses quoted in this book were referenced from the King James Version (KJV), New King James Version (NKJV), and the New International Version (NIV).

FEEDBACK

Please write to us and tell us if *Tiers of Sorrow* impacted you or someone you know.

www.SandraToscanoBooks.com.

www.Instagram.com/SandraToscanoBooks

www.Facebook.com/SandraToscanoBooks

RECOMMENDED BOOKS

Code Of the Forest
Jon Buchan

My Life After Hate
Arno Arr Michaels

His Kingdom Come
Margaret Montreuil

FourBears: The Myth of Forgiveness
Sammy Rangel

Mom—In Honor of Good Mothers
Wayne Coster Cooper

Mosaic Cross
WritersInTheSpirit

The Pilgrim Strain
C.P. Edgar

www.ingramcontent.com/pod-product-compliance
Lightning Source LLC
Chambersburg PA
CBHW021924040426
42448CB00008B/898